100
BEST
VEGAN
RECIPES

ROBIN ROBERTSON

PHOTOGRAPHS BY
LUCY SCHAEFFER

HOUGHTON MIFFLIN HARCOURT
BOSTON • NEW YORK • 2016

For information about permission to reproduce selections from
this book, write to trade.permissions@hmhco.com or to Permissions,
Houghton Mifflin Harcourt Publishing Company, 3 Park Avenue,
19th Floor, New York, New York 10016.

www.hmhco.com

Library of Congress Cataloging-in-Publication Data
Robertson, Robin (Robin G.)
  100 best vegan recipes / Robin Robertson.
      pages cm
  ISBN 978-0-544-43969-6 (hardcover) — ISBN 978-0-544-43970-2 (ebook)
1. Vegan cooking. I. Title. II. Title: One hundred best vegan recipes.
  TX837.R62364 2015
  641.5'636 — dc23
          2015027945

Printed in China
C&C 10 9 8 7 6 5 4 3 2 1

Publisher: Natalie Chapman
Executive Editor: Anne Ficklen
Editorial Assistant: Martha Wydysh
Associate Production Editor: Helen Seachrist
Cover and Interior Design: Chrissy Kurpeski
Manufacturing Manager: Kevin Watt

For the animals

Contents

Introduction

In *100 Best Vegan Recipes* you will find many of the most-loved dishes from *1,000 Vegan Recipes* (including fan favorites), plus several all-new recipes to complete the list. The only thing more challenging than writing a cookbook containing a thousand recipes was deciding which of those recipes to feature in this "100 Best" collection. While some people are still amazed by a cookbook with 1,000 recipes that uses no animal products of any kind, the fact is, there are countless ways to prepare delicious plant-based food. Ultimately, I chose mostly main-dish recipes to answer the perennial question we all have every day: "What's for dinner?" In addition, I have included a selection of go-to dessert and breakfast recipes to show how easy (and delicious) it is to cook and bake without dairy and eggs. And what would a cookbook be without some great soups, sandwiches, salads, and sides?

Among the new recipes featured in this book are: Cheesy Rice Balls (page 30), Carrot Super-Slaw with Edamame and Almonds (page 76), Kale and Red Beans with Olives and Lemon (page 99), Buffalo-Style Kale Crisps (page 28), Creamy Artichoke and Spinach Gemelli (page 115), Bánh Mì Tostadas (page 61), Provençal Burgers (page 64), and Chimichurri White Beans and Roasted Asparagus (page 92).

These recipes are designed to appeal to cooks of all skill levels and abilities, from seasoned cooks to novices. With clear instructions and easy-to-find ingredients, the recipes in *100 Best Vegan Recipes* deliver delicious dishes to satisfy a variety of tastes and occasions. The recipes include global ethnic favorites, such as Pad Thai at Home (page 124) and Linguine Puttanesca (page 113), and family-style comfort foods such as Millet-Topped Lentil Shepherd's Pie (page 110) and One-Dish Dauphinoise (page 130). Even meat eaters will enjoy flavorful and satisfying dishes such as Red Bean Jambalaya (page 109), Broccoli- and Cheddar-Stuffed Portobellos (page 160), and Brazilian Black Bean Stew (page 54).

Among the many tempting appetizers in this book are Artichoke-Walnut Squares (page 31), Mango-Avocado Summer Rolls (page 34), and Smoky Chipotle-Pinto Hummus (page 37), as well as some stunning side dishes such as Curry-Roasted Cauliflower (page 148) and Emerald Mashed Potatoes (page 155). Scrumptious desserts include Agave Baklava (page 178), Sour Cream Coffee Cake (page 177), and Double-Chocolate Brownies (page 180).

People who are new to plant-based cooking often discover that the world is suddenly bigger, not smaller. They find a new range of ingredients, such as tofu, tempeh, and seitan, and a previously overlooked world of beans and grains. They are also pleased to discover many naturally vegan dishes from around the world where plant-based meals have been enjoyed for centuries, both for their good taste and their healthfulness.

With an emphasis on fresh, whole foods, the recipes in *100 Best Vegan Recipes* are cholesterol-free, low in saturated fat, and high in fiber and complex carbohydrates. Most importantly, these delicious recipes will help make menu planning a breeze and dinner a hearty, flavorful, and simply delectable experience. To me, vegan cooking is a celebration of the world's diverse cultures, an homage to good health, and a way to honor and respect all life. Whether you're savoring a bite of Roasted Vegetable Lasagna (page 112) or devouring the last piece of Crazy for Carrot Cake (page 175), I hope you'll enjoy *100 Best Vegan Recipes* as a glimpse of the variety available in the vast world of vegan cooking.

A Vegan Kitchen

Welcome to my special collection of top recipes from *1,000 Vegan Recipes*, plus a few new ones to enjoy. If you are reading this, you are probably already vegan, trying to improve your health by seeking alternatives to meat and dairy in your diet, or a traditional eater incorporating some plant-based options into your routine. Whatever the case, I hope you'll enjoy these recipes. I've developed them to be as delicious and satisfying as anything in the non-vegan world so that anyone in your household can enjoy them.

Before we dig into the recipes, let's go over some basics for keeping a vegan kitchen, including ingredient information and tips you'll find helpful along the way.

How to Make Great Food Simply

For some cooks, approaching a recipe is intimidating, but it shouldn't be. Even if you've been cooking for a long time, consider these tips whenever you cook.

- **Get the recipe in your head.** Before starting any recipe, read the recipe through like it's a newspaper article, and then read it again, making notes on any ingredients you do not have on hand. This becomes your shopping list.
- *Mise-en-place.* Once you have all the ingredients you need, gather them together along with any equipment you may need. This process, *mise-en-place*, includes preheating your oven as well as chopping and pre-measuring ingredients in the quantities required. Then, you are ready to cook. This way, you won't be scrambling for a spatula or chopping an onion while your oil is burning. It can also help you avoid discovering missing ingredients, get done faster, and enjoy the cooking process.
- **Let the new ingredients become your new staples.** If you're trying plant-based cooking for the first time, you're likely to suddenly discover that your culinary world has gotten bigger, not smaller. Let the new

ingredients become your new staples. If you're new to plant-based cooking, you may be pleased to discover lots of delicious "new to you" ingredients, from almond milk and tofu, to flax seeds and nutritional yeast. Have fun exploring and expanding your culinary horizons.

- **Explore the world from your kitchen.** You may also be very pleased to discover a host of naturally vegan dishes from other geographic areas, such as India, the Middle East, Mexico, Indonesia, the Mediterranean, and Asia, where plant-based ingredients have been used for centuries for their great flavors and health value.

Six Steps to a Successful Plant-Based Diet

If you are new to veganism, use the following guidelines to help you make the transition to a plant-based diet:

1. List your current favorite dishes, then substitute beans, tofu, tempeh, or another plant-based protein for the meat used in them—it's easy to make ingredient swaps!
2. Think of vegetable dishes as your entrées instead of side dishes. Add beans to make a more substantial meal.
3. Prepare two or three new vegan recipes every week. Soon, you will have a full repertoire to rotate and keep your meals interesting.
4. Use nondairy milk and vegan butter (try Earth Balance brand) at breakfast and for baking.
5. Keep your pantry well stocked with plant-based ingredients so there's always a way to prepare a great vegan meal.
6. When dining out, choose restaurants that offer vegan options. Many Asian restaurants will make anything on their menus with tofu, and Indian restaurants serve delicious bean and vegetable dishes.

GOOD HEALTH IS ALL ABOUT BALANCED NUTRITION

Enough has been said about fast food, junk food, and foods derived from meat and dairy. Scientific studies show that a plant-based diet that includes lots of fresh produce, beans, and whole grains can improve our health in a number of ways. However, if even the most committed vegan neglects his or her diet or forgets to maintain a proper balance of nutrients, ill health can also be the result—a diet of potato chips and celery may be vegan, but it's never going to keep you healthy. Poor health can occur particularly with people who choose to become vegan but don't take the time to form new habits for cooking and eating.

As with any style of cooking, a commonsense understanding of basic nutrition is important. The key to a plant-based diet is eating a variety of (as fresh as possible) vegetables, whole grains, legumes, nuts, seeds, and fruits each day in order to acquire the nutrients necessary for good health, including protein, calcium, fat, and iron.

PLANT-BASED PROTEIN

One of the questions vegans are most frequently asked is, "Where do you get your protein?" Longtime vegans already know the answer to that, but it's worth a review.

A wide variety of whole foods contain protein, including beans, whole grains, fruits, vegetables, nuts, and seeds, along with products derived from them, such as tofu, tempeh, and quality meat-alternative products. Medical authorities maintain that if you eat a reasonably varied vegan diet and ingest enough calories, you will get enough protein.

Many people don't realize this, but whole grains, beans, and vegetables contain various amounts and quality levels of protein and their essential amino acids. All beans do not provide complete protein, but soybeans surpass all other food plants in the amount of protein they deliver. Many vegan meals pair grains and beans together, so this is an ideal way to get all the nutrients you need. If you eat a variety of wholesome plant-based ingredients daily, along with some fresh vegetables and fruits, it will go a long way toward helping you maintain good health.

The plant-based diet provides calcium in tofu, dark leafy

greens, sesame seeds, almonds, and cooked beans. Look no further than tofu, lentils, beans, tahini, and grains for iron. Vitamin B12 can be found in nutritional yeast, fortified cereals, fortified soy milk, tempeh, and miso. Omega-3s are found in adequate amounts in vegetables, fruits, beans, and, most notably, flaxseeds.

REPLACING DAIRY PRODUCTS

People who have difficulty making the transition to a plant-based diet often remain "vegetarian" because it's difficult for them to part with products such as milk, cheese, and eggs. Fortunately, a variety of plant-based alternatives are now available that facilitate baking (see page 21 for tips on replacing eggs in baking) and cooking all your favorite creamy dishes.

Among all the nondairy milks now available, soy milk contains the highest concentration of protein. Such "milks" can be purchased (or made) from soy, rice, oats, and various nuts. These milks are available in most supermarkets and natural foods stores. Some even come flavored as vanilla or chocolate. Vegan mayonnaise, such as the very excellent Just Mayo and Vegenaise, is also available, as well as dairy-free sour cream, cream cheese, and other kinds of "cheese," made from soy, rice, or other plant-based ingredients.

In the place of butter, choose high-quality expeller-pressed or cold-pressed oils, which are made without the use of heat and harsh solvents. For a solid butter alternative, I recommend Earth Balance brand buttery spread. On your morning toast, consider using nut butters. While they contain about the same amount of calories as butter, they provide plenty of protein and essential fatty acids without any bad cholesterol.

INGREDIENTS TO KNOW AND LOVE

If you want to look younger, trim down, have clearer skin, and enjoy more energy, then a well-balanced plant-based diet is for you. A vegan diet keeps your heart healthy and lowers the risk of cancer. Fresh, whole foods are loaded with vitamins, nutrients, and protein, as well as antioxidants, minerals, and calcium. They contain no cholesterol and are low in saturated fats.

Tofu

Tofu is one of the best protein sources on earth and lends itself well to a variety of dishes and cooking methods because it absorbs the surrounding flavors. Also known as bean curd, tofu is curdled soy milk, extracted from ground, cooked soybeans, and made in a process similar to the way cheese is made. Tofu is available in two main types: regular (Chinese) and silken (Japanese). Both types come in three textures: soft, firm, and extra-firm.

Extra-firm regular tofu is the sturdiest and works well in stir-fries and other dishes in which the tofu must retain its shape. Soft regular tofu is used in recipes where a softer texture is desired, such as in lasagna, where it functions like ricotta, but in which silken tofu would be too soft. Regular tofu is also available marinated and baked in several flavors and can be used as is, without additional seasoning. I think of it as a protein-rich convenience food. Cube it and add to salads and stir-fries, or slice it and add to sandwiches and wraps. Silken tofu, or Japanese-style tofu, is used when the desired result is smooth and creamy, such as in smoothies, sauces, and desserts.

Always drain tofu before using. Blot it and press out the excess water. To squeeze tofu dry, cut the block into slabs and place the slabs on a baking sheet or cutting board lined with paper towels or a clean kitchen towel. Top the tofu with another towel, then top with another baking sheet. Weigh down the top baking sheet with a heavy skillet or canned goods and let it sit for an hour.

Regular tofu can be frozen, but its texture will become chewy and more porous, which works well for marinating or sautéing. Freezing also makes tofu easier to crumble for use in recipes such as chili. To freeze tofu, cut the drained and pressed tofu into slices and either place in an airtight container or wrap in plastic wrap. When needed for a recipe, thaw the tofu and squeeze again to remove excess water. Frozen, tofu will keep for several months. Once defrosted, tofu should be used within two to three days.

Tempeh

Originally from Indonesia, tempeh is made from fermented, compressed soybeans and is especially well suited to stews, stir-fries, and sautés because, like tofu, it absorbs the surrounding flavors. Tempeh turns a crisp golden brown when fried, and it marinates well. Tempeh is high in protein, with a chewy texture.

Tempeh can be found in the refrigerated or freezer sections of natural foods stores, Asian markets, and some supermarkets, and is usually sold in 8-ounce slabs. The slabs can be sliced lengthwise to make thin slices and can also be cut into strips, cubed, or grated. Tempeh requires refrigeration and will keep, unopened, for several weeks (always check the expiration date). Once it is opened, however, it should be wrapped tightly and used within three days. Tempeh will keep for a month or so frozen. As tempeh can have a strong nutty flavor, I recommend steaming it for 30 minutes before using, to mellow the flavor and aid digestibility.

Wheat Meat or Seitan

Seitan, as it is known in Japan, is the gluten that remains after washing the starch and bran from whole wheat flour. It is perhaps the most versatile ingredient owing to its chewy texture and the forms it can take. It can be diced, cut into strips for stir-fries, cubed for stews and soups, shredded or ground, stuffed like a roast, or thinly sliced. Dining on a meal of seitan, meat consumers may have a change of heart about plant-based dishes.

Making homemade seitan is fairly easy, and a recipe for doing so is included in this book. To save time, you can purchase precooked seitan in natural foods stores and Asian markets. Always read the label, as commercial seitan sometimes comes marinated, and the flavors may be incompatible with your recipe. Also be sure to drain and rinse marinated seitan.

Other Protein Choices

In addition to tofu, wheat meat (seitan), and tempeh, a number of commercial plant-based products are made to mimic, in taste and texture, actual meat products such as burgers and sausages. Some vegans avoid commercial meat and dairy alternative products for a number of reasons. Others find them useful, especially when making the transition to a plant-based diet or cooking for finicky children.

I do not call for commercial meat-alternative products in *100 Best Vegan Recipes*. However, a small number of the recipes, such as jambalaya, reference ingredients like vegan sausage links as an optional ingredient.

Beans

All around the world, people rely on beans as their main source of protein. They are inexpensive, easy to use, low in fat, and a vital component of any well-balanced plant-based diet. Whether you're cooking chickpeas, black-eyed peas, lentils, black beans, pintos, kidney beans, limas, or cannellini, beans are high in protein, fiber, complex carbohydrates, and B vitamins. Beans find their way into stews, burgers, loaves, spreads, and more. Dried beans require a soaking step before they can be used, but you can cut your prep time by using organic canned beans. If you want to use dried beans, however, follow the basic instructions provided on the next page.

Soaking and Cooking Beans

Dried beans (except for lentils and split peas) should be soaked before cooking. Soaking rehydrates the beans and shortens their cooking time. It also dissolves some of the complex sugars that cause digestive gas. Before soaking, pick through the dried beans to remove small stones and sticks.

To soak: Place the beans in a bowl with enough water to cover by 3 inches. Soak overnight, and drain before cooking. To quick-soak beans, put them in a pot under 2 to 3 inches of water and boil for 2 minutes. Remove the pot from the stove, cover it, and let it stand for 2 hours. Drain the beans, and they're ready for cooking.

To cook: Simmer 1 cup of beans in 3 cups of water over low heat until tender. Salt and acidic ingredients such as tomatoes should be added at the end of the cooking time, as salt will toughen the beans if added too soon. Generally, 1 cup of dried beans yields 2 to 2½ cups of cooked beans. Cooking times will vary, depending on the type, quality, and age of the beans. Altitude and water quality can also vary the results.

Grains

Grains are a dependable staple throughout the world. They are abundant, inexpensive, great sources of protein and fiber, and have more complex carbohydrates than any other food. From breakfast cereal to daily bread, grains find their way into every diet. In vegan cooking, however, we learn how to use the global pantry of whole grains for high nutrition and their variety of textures and flavors.

Before you cook any grains, be sure to rinse them to remove loose hulls, dust, and other impurities. Whenever I want to intensify the flavor, I lightly toast the grains in a dry skillet before cooking.

Cooking Grains

Pour the grain into a pot and cover with twice as much water. Bring the water to a boil, then decrease the heat to low and simmer until tender. The cooking time will vary according to the type of grain. Wait until the water boils to add the salt. After cooking, let the pot stand, covered, for 5 minutes before serving. By the time it's done, the water should be entirely absorbed. When ready to serve, fluff the grain with a fork. One cup of uncooked grain makes about 3 cups of cooked grain.

Grains can also be baked in the oven in a tightly covered pot, cooked in a pressure cooker, or, as in the case of pilaf, prepared in a skillet on top of the stove. For this method, sauté the grains in oil first, then add liquids and cook until tender.

Vegetables

Every day, you can enjoy nutritious, satisfying plant-based dishes made from protein-rich beans, grains, nuts, and soy foods combined with fresh, organic produce. Whenever possible, use fresh, locally grown vegetables, and be sure to take advantage of the variety that may be available. Vegetables are now the featured stars, not the side-dish bit players, so choose them at their peak of freshness. To make sure you are getting full nutrition in your diet, be magnanimous. Combine veggies in pleasing color combinations, and be sure to include leafy greens, root vegetables, and squashes, too.

Nuts and Seeds

Nuts and seeds can be enjoyed in both sweet and savory dishes. Important sources of protein for vegans, nuts and seeds can be found in and out of the shell, whole, halved, sliced, chopped, raw, roasted, or made into nut butters. Studies show that just 2 ounces of almonds, pecans, or other nuts each day can dramatically lower harmful LDL cholesterol. Due to their high oil content, nuts and seeds go rancid once the shells are removed, so they should be refrigerated in airtight containers. Properly stored, they will keep for several months.

A wide variety of nut butters are available, including almond, cashew, hazelnut, macadamia, pistachio, tahini (sesame paste), and even soy. They are rich in protein, fiber, and essential fatty acids. Nut butters work well in vegan cooking because they can be used to make sauces, to enrich soups and stews, and as a healthy fat replacement in baking. They are easier to digest than whole nuts and can be made at home with a blender. They, too, should be kept refrigerated in covered jars, where they will keep for as long as a month. Try to buy only natural nut butters, which do not contain stabilizers and other additives.

OTHER IMPORTANT INGREDIENTS

Oils

Buy organic oils labeled either cold-pressed, unrefined, or expeller-pressed. I use extra-virgin olive oil whenever possible because of its good flavor and health benefits. It's especially good on salads and pasta dishes, and can be used in moderate-temperature cooking. I never use olive oil for higher-temperature cooking, such as in an Asian stir-fry, as it becomes unstable. Moreover, the olive flavor may compete with other ingredients. I reserve a pricier extra-virgin olive oil for salads or drizzling on a cooked dish for added flavor and use a less expensive type for cooking.

For a flavorless oil that is stable at higher temperatures, use either grapeseed oil or safflower oil. To impart an Asian flavor to salads and other recipes, use dark (toasted) sesame oil. This flavorful oil is used for seasoning, not cooking, since it, too, becomes unstable at high temperatures. A little goes a long way.

Flaxseed oil, a great source of omega-3 fatty acids, has heart-healthy properties and various other nutritional benefits. Don't use flaxseed oil for cooking, but incorporate some in salads and smoothies for added omega-3s.

Salt

Salt can be the deciding factor in whether a dish is flavorful or bland. I use sea salt for general use, because it's natural, balances flavors, and contributes to nutrition. Ordinary table salt tastes bitter, has no nutrition, and contains chemicals to prevent caking. To avoid excess sodium (as opposed to salt for flavoring), try to cook with natural whole foods; use a low-sodium soy sauce; and when using canned beans, look for an organic variety, since they contain less sodium. Add salt to a dish while it is cooking rather than afterward to allow the salt to dissolve and incorporate into the food.

Soy Sauce

In many dishes in which soy sauce is used, the sauce itself provides the salt content. However, some soy sauces are very high in sodium and additives, which can result in a bitter or harsh flavor. For best results, I recommend high-quality, reduced-sodium soy sauces, as well as shoyu and tamari. They do contain some salt, but they are naturally fermented and mellower in flavor.

Vegetable Broth

For great vegan soups and sauces, use a good vegetable broth. Broth adds rich flavor to any recipes that call for broth or water and boosts nutrition, too. If you don't have time to make homemade broth, you can buy vegetable broth in cans or aseptic containers. As a substitute, you can use a powdered or paste vegetable soup base or bouillon cubes. The salt content in these products varies, so find one you like and adjust seasonings accordingly. Some commercial broths are so rich and intense that I cut them with water by half and freeze what I don't use.

It's not difficult to make a quick, simple broth. Add washed, coarsely chopped vegetables to the water and let it simmer for an hour. Strain out the vegetables, and the result is a good, simple broth. Even an all-purpose broth made with some basics such as carrots, celery, onions, and water will add dimension to your cooking. For a richer broth, I coarsely chop the vegetables, with their leaves, skins, peels, and stems, and sweat them in a little oil to bring out their flavors before adding water.

ABOUT SWEETENERS

In cooking, I use an unrefined sugar, or naturally processed granulated sugarcane, which is sold under various brand names, such as Florida Crystals. These can be substituted in equal measure for white table sugar. Since honey is not vegan, substitute agave nectar or pure maple syrup, though maple will always add a bit of its distinct flavor to whatever you're cooking. Both have a similar sweetness level as honey.

VEGAN BAKING

Most types of baked goods can easily be made plant-based by replacing the dairy and eggs in traditional recipes with vegan ingredients. Some of the obvious substitutions are: soy milk or almond milk to replace dairy milk; non-hydrogenated vegan butter or oil instead of dairy butter; and agave nectar or pure maple syrup to replace honey. Various companies now make dairy-free semisweet chocolate.

Many shortcut baking products are also vegan, such as prepared phyllo dough and puff pastry, as well as many prepared piecrusts (although some brands contain lard, so be sure to check the label). If you prefer to bake something "almost from scratch," there are a number of vegan baking mixes available. (Check online for sources.)

In the meantime, there are lots of ways to replace eggs in baking. Use any of these techniques to replace 1 egg in a baking recipe:

- **Applesauce:** Blend ¼ cup applesauce with ½ teaspoon baking powder.
- **Arrowroot:** Blend 2 tablespoons arrowroot in a blender with 3 tablespoons water.
- **Baking powder:** Blend 2 tablespoons baking powder with 2 tablespoons water and 1 tablespoon oil.

- **Banana Puree:** ½ banana with ½ teaspoon baking powder.
- **Chia seeds:** Combine 1 tablespoon chia seeds with ¼ to ⅓ cup water in a bowl and set aside for 15 minutes.
- **Chickpea flour:** Blend 3 tablespoons chickpea flour with 3 tablespoons water.
- **Ener-G Egg Replacer:** Blend 1¼ teaspoons of the powder with 3 tablespoons water.
- **Flaxseeds:** Process 1 tablespoon ground flaxseeds plus 3 tablespoons water in a blender for 1 to 2 minutes, until the mixture becomes viscous.
- **Nut butter:** Use 3 tablespoons creamy nut butter (at room temperature).
- **Tofu:** Combine ¼ cup drained soft or silken tofu and ½ teaspoon baking powder.

STOCKING YOUR VEGAN PANTRY

To make plant-based cooking convenient and fun, acquire a basic vegan pantry that includes a variety of beans, grains, pastas, and tomato products, along with tahini, salsa, peanut butter, and chutney, all of which add to your creativity in the kitchen.

Certain highly perishable ingredients are vital to a vegan pantry. These include fresh fruits and vegetables, seeds, nuts, whole-grain flours, and oils, which can turn rancid. So, after being opened, it's best to get these out of the pantry and into the refrigerator. Other ingredients to keep on hand are dried herbs, spices, vinegars, sea salt, and other basic seasonings, as well as baking items such as flour, baking powder, baking soda, extracts, and thickeners.

Fresh ingredients are also important to the list, so if you are not already in the habit, keep onions, celery, and carrots in the fridge drawer, along with fresh lettuce and other salad fixings and a variety of vegetables and fruits. Have on hand lemons, limes, garlic, fresh ginger, olives, and fresh herbs whenever available. Also keep handy tofu, tempeh, seitan, veggie burgers, and other products you may use, such as vegan sour cream, tofu cream cheese, and vegan mayonnaise. There is no need to stock every item all the time, but choose the items you will regularly use, and purchase others as you need them.

NOTES ON THE RECIPES

These recipes are designed to be user friendly, with simple instructions, easy-to-find ingredients, and substitution suggestions for ingredients that may be difficult to find or not in season. Still, there are a few points to clarify in order for you to get the best results from these recipes.

Can Sizes
When ingredients such as beans or tomatoes list a can size, I've used the size that I find in my local supermarket. Since brands can vary from store to store, you should use whatever is closest in size to that listed. For example, the canned beans I buy are almost all 15.5-ounce cans (about 1½ cups when drained). If your cans are 16 ounces and yield closer to 2 cups, go ahead and use them—such a small difference in volume will be insignificant to the success of the recipes.

Seasoning with Salt to Taste
When a recipe says "season with salt to taste" rather than an actual measurement, it usually has to do with the relative saltiness of the other ingredients in the recipe, such as vegetable broth, which can range from unsalted to very salty. The key here is "to taste." Tasting as you prepare a recipe is an important element of good cooking because it allows you to keep the seasonings in check.

Substituting Ingredients
Whether for personal taste, allergies, or other reasons, there may be some ingredients used in recipes that you can't or don't want to use. Think of a recipe as a road map designed to help you find your way to a destination—in this case, great-tasting food. Whether you take the direct route (following the recipe exactly) or try a few side roads

(by substituting ingredients or changing the recipe in some way to suit your taste) matters little, as long as the results are pleasing. So if a recipe calls for cilantro and you don't like it, leave it out or use parsley instead. If you're not a fan of chickpeas, use a bean variety you do enjoy, and so on. You'll enjoy cooking more if you are flexible, creative, and relaxed.

Washing Your Produce

In every case, the recipes in this book assume that you have thoroughly washed, scrubbed, or trimmed all the produce before using it in the recipes. Fruits and vegetables should be well scrubbed in general before using them in order to rinse off pesticides and bacteria. Leafy greens need to be thoroughly washed to remove sand and grit. Potatoes and root vegetables should be well scrubbed as well, and any wilted or damaged areas should be removed before using them.

Kitchen Equipment

With so many choices available, kitchen equipment can be costly and confusing. As much as I like the newest, latest gadgets, I also know that you can cook up a storm with a minimum of basic, reliable equipment.

Where cookware is concerned, quality is definitely better than quantity. If you're short on space or cash, it's better to have a few good multipurpose saucepans and pots, a good skillet, and a few good knives than a kitchen full of trendy gadgets. A good 12-inch skillet, for example, can be used to sauté, braise, and stir-fry. A large pot can be used for soups and stews or as a pasta pot. One or two saucepans can take care of the rest.

If you can't afford a full set of knives, opt for a good 8-inch chef's knife, a 4-inch paring knife, and a serrated knife. Add to that list a colander, mixing bowls, baking pans, a good cutting board, and a food processor or blender, and you can cook your way through just about any culinary scenario.

Enjoy

I invite you to try these recipes once or twice a week over the next several months. That way, you'll discover favorites the way thousands of my readers have over the years. With plant-based cooking, you can make roasts without meat, sandwiches without cold cuts, cream sauces without cream, cheesecakes without cheese, and cakes without eggs.

Go-To Snacks and Apps

It's always a good idea to have a few go-to appetizers and snacks in your culinary arsenal. Whether you favor simple dips with chips or lean toward tapas or pâté, this collection of tasty bites has got you covered.

Buffalo-Style Kale Crisps

MAKES ABOUT 4 CUPS

Crispy kale makes a great side dish or snack. You can enjoy the chips plain, tossed with nutritional yeast, sprinkled with your favorite herbs or seasonings, or made spicy like these Buffalo-style crisps.

- 1 **bunch kale**
- ½ **cup raw cashews, soaked for 3 hours, then drained**
- ½ **cup diced red bell pepper**
- 2 **tablespoons nutritional yeast**
- ¼ **cup hot sauce (such as Frank's Red Hot)**
- 1 **teaspoon smoked paprika**
- 1 **teaspoon chipotle chile powder (optional)**
- ½ **teaspoon sea salt**

1. Remove any thick stems from the kale. Wash the kale leaves well, then dry them well in a salad spinner or in a clean dish towel—they should be very dry. Tear or cut any large leaves into 2-inch pieces. Preheat the oven to 350°F. Line two large baking sheets with parchment paper. Set aside.

2. In a food processor or high-speed blender, combine the cashews, bell pepper, nutritional yeast, hot sauce, paprika, chipotle chile powder (if using), and salt. Process until smooth. The sauce should be thick, but if it's too thick, add a little water, 1 tablespoon at a time.

3. Transfer the kale leaves to a bowl. Pour on the sauce and toss to coat, massaging the sauce into the leaves. Arrange the kale in a single layer on the prepared baking sheets. Bake for 20 minutes. Remove any pieces that are crisp and turn over any pieces that are not crisp, then return to the oven until crisp, watching so they don't burn, 5 to 10 minutes longer.

Black Bean and Sun-Dried Tomato Dip

MAKES ABOUT 1 ½ CUPS

Sun-dried tomatoes and balsamic vinegar add a complexity to the flavor of this robust dip. Serve with whole-grain crackers or toasted coarse bread.

- ¼ cup reconstituted or oil-packed sun-dried tomatoes
- 1½ cups cooked or 1 (15.5-ounce) can black beans, drained and rinsed
- 1 tablespoon balsamic vinegar
- 2 tablespoons chopped fresh parsley
- ¼ teaspoon dried marjoram or basil
- Salt and freshly ground black pepper

In a food processor, process the tomatoes until finely chopped. Add the beans and pulse just long enough to break them up a bit. Add the vinegar, parsley, marjoram, and salt and pepper to taste. Process until just blended, leaving some texture.

Cheesy Rice Balls

SERVES 4

Golden orbs of cheesy rice dipped in warm marinara sauce makes a delicious hot appetizer for an Italian meal. Be sure to plan ahead so the cashews have enough time to soak and the rice has enough time to chill before proceeding with the recipe.

½ cup raw cashews, soaked for 3 hours, then drained
1 tablespoon roasted red bell pepper or jarred pimientos, blotted dry
1 garlic clove, crushed
1 tablespoon cider vinegar
1 tablespoon water or dry white wine
½ teaspoon dark brown mustard
2 tablespoons nutritional yeast
¼ teaspoon salt
¼ teaspoon onion powder
¼ teaspoon smoked paprika
   Pinch of ground turmeric
2 cups well-cooked (soft) brown rice
⅓ cup finely minced scallions
¼ cup ground walnuts or dried bread crumbs
¼ cup cornstarch
   Grapeseed oil, for frying
   Marinara sauce, warmed, for serving

1. In a food processor or high-speed blender, combine the cashews, roasted red bell pepper, garlic, vinegar, water, and mustard. Process until smooth. Add the nutritional yeast, salt, onion powder, paprika, and turmeric. Process until smooth, scraping down the sides as needed.

2. Scrape the mixture into a bowl. Add the cooked rice and scallions. Mix well. Refrigerate for 2 hours to firm up, then roll the mixture into 1½-inch balls.

3. Combine the walnuts with the cornstarch in a shallow bowl and mix to combine. Roll each rice ball in the walnut mixture. Heat a thin layer of oil in a nonstick skillet. Add the rice balls, a few at a time, and cook until nicely browned, 2 to 3 minutes, turning as needed. Repeat until all the rice balls are cooked. Serve warm or at room temperature with warm marinara sauce.

Artichoke-Walnut Squares

MAKES 16 SQUARES

Studded with pieces of marinated artichoke hearts and topped with ground walnuts, these delicious squares are easy to prepare and can be made ahead, then reheated in a moderate oven or served at room temperature. If cooking for a crowd, this recipe is easily doubled.

- ¼ cup plus 1 tablespoon olive oil
- 1 large yellow onion, chopped
- 2 garlic cloves, minced
- ½ teaspoon dried thyme
  Salt and freshly ground black pepper
- 1 (12-ounce) jar marinated artichoke hearts, drained and chopped
- 1½ cups all-purpose flour
- 2 tablespoons nutritional yeast
- 2 teaspoons baking powder
- 2 tablespoons chopped fresh parsley
- ¾ cup plain unsweetened almond milk
- 2 tablespoons fresh lemon juice
- ½ cup ground walnuts

1. Preheat the oven to 425°F. Heat 1 tablespoon of the oil in a skillet over medium heat. Add the onion, cover, and cook until softened, 5 minutes. Stir in the garlic and thyme. Season with salt and pepper to taste and cook for 30 seconds, then remove from the heat, stir in the artichokes, and set aside to cool.

2. In a bowl, combine the flour, nutritional yeast, baking powder, and 1 teaspoon salt. Add the remaining ¼ cup oil and stir until the mixture resembles coarse crumbs. Add the parsley, almond milk and stir to combine. Stir in the artichoke and onion mixture and half of the walnuts.

3. Spread the mixture evenly over the bottom of a lightly oiled 8-inch square pan. Sprinkle the top with the remaining walnuts. Bake until hot and cooked through, about 30 minutes. Allow to cool slightly before cutting into squares. Serve warm or at room temperature.

Mushrooms Stuffed with Spinach and Walnuts

SERVES 4

These juicy mushrooms are stuffed with a flavorful mixture of spinach, walnuts, and garlic. Delicious and easy to make, they can be arranged on a platter as a pick-up food or nestled on small plates to serve as an appetizer for a special dinner.

   2 **tablespoons olive oil**
   1 **pound white mushroom caps, stems reserved**
   1 **garlic clove, minced**
   1 **cup chopped cooked spinach**
   1 **cup finely chopped walnuts**
   ½ **cup dried bread crumbs**
      Salt and freshly ground black pepper

1. Preheat the oven to 400°F and lightly oil a baking pan large enough to fit the mushroom caps in a single layer. Heat the oil in a large skillet over medium heat. Add the mushroom caps and cook for 2 minutes to soften slightly. Remove from the skillet and set aside.

2. Chop the mushroom stems and add to the same skillet. Add the garlic and cook over medium heat until softened, about 2 minutes. Squeeze any excess water from the spinach, then add the spinach to the skillet along with the walnuts, bread crumbs, and salt and pepper to taste. Cook for 2 minutes, stirring well to combine.

3. Fill the mushroom caps with the stuffing mixture and arrange in a single layer in the baking pan. Bake until the mushrooms are tender and the filling is hot, about 10 minutes. Serve hot.

Mango-Avocado Summer Rolls

MAKES 10 TO 12 ROLLS

Serve these refreshing summer rolls with the Mango-Ponzu Sauce or your favorite dipping sauce. Look for rice paper wrappers and rice vermicelli at Asian markets, well-stocked supermarkets, or online.

  3 ounces rice vermicelli or bean thread noodles
 12 rice paper wrappers
  2 ripe Hass avocados
  1 tablespoon fresh lemon juice
  1 ripe mango, peeled, pitted, and cut lengthwise into ¼-inch strips
  1 English cucumber, peeled, halved lengthwise, seeded,
       and cut into thin strips
  2 cups finely sliced romaine or iceberg lettuce
     Salt and freshly ground black pepper
 ½ cup fresh cilantro leaves
     Mango-Ponzu Sauce (recipe follows), for serving

1. Soak the noodles in hot water until transparent, about 1 minute, and drain well. Cut the noodles into 4-inch lengths and set aside in a bowl.

2. Fill a large shallow bowl with warm water and add one rice paper wrapper, soaking it in the water for just a few seconds until soft. Remove it from the water and lay it on a dry cutting board.

3. Peel and pit the avocados and cut them into ¼-inch strips. Toss the avocado strips with the lemon juice to avoid discoloration, then place 2 or 3 avocado strips down the center of the wrapper, leaving a 1-inch margin at each end of the wrapper. Top with a few strips of mango, followed by a layer of cucumber strips. Top with some of the rice vermicelli and a layer of lettuce strips. Season with salt and pepper and sprinkle with some of the cilantro leaves. Pull one side of the rice paper over the filling, folding over the two short ends, rolling up tightly to enclose the filling. Transfer to a serving plate and repeat with the remaining wrappers and filling ingredients. Serve immediately, with the dipping sauce, or cover the rolls with a damp cloth for no more than 1 hour before serving.

CONTINUED ON PAGE 36

CONTINUED FROM PAGE 34

Mango-Ponzu Sauce

MAKES ABOUT 1 CUP

Ponzu sauce is a citrusy Japanese cooking liquid available in well-stocked supermarkets, Asian markets, and gourmet grocers.

- 1 cup diced ripe mango
- 2 tablespoons water
- 1 tablespoon ponzu sauce
- 2 teaspoons soy sauce
- ¼ teaspoon sriracha sauce
- ¼ teaspoon sugar

1. Combine all of the ingredients in a blender and blend until smooth, adding more water if needed to achieve a sauce-like consistency.

2. Transfer to a small serving bowl. If not using right away, cover with plastic wrap and refrigerate until ready to use.

Smoky Chipotle-Pinto Hummus

MAKES ABOUT 1½ CUPS

Pinto beans and spicy chipotle chiles combine to create a hummus-inspired dip that goes great with tortilla chips.

- 1 garlic clove, crushed
- 1½ cups cooked or 1 (15.5-ounce) can pinto beans, drained and rinsed
- 1½ teaspoons canned chipotle chiles in adobo sauce
- 2 teaspoons fresh lime juice
  Salt and freshly ground black pepper
- 1 tablespoon finely minced scallions

1. Mince the garlic in a food processor. Add the pinto beans and chipotle and process until smooth. Add the lime juice and salt and pepper to taste. Process until well blended.

2. Transfer to a bowl and sprinkle with the scallions. Serve right away, or cover and refrigerate for an hour or two to allow the flavors to intensify.

Smooth and Savory Mushroom Pâté

MAKES ABOUT 1 1⁄2 CUPS

Ground cashews give this luxurious pâté a buttery richness that will make it disappear quickly. Serve with a selection of crackers or breads for slathering.

- 1 tablespoon olive oil
- 1⁄2 cup chopped onion
- 1 garlic clove, minced
- 2 cups sliced mushrooms
- 1⁄2 teaspoon dried savory or thyme
- 1 tablespoon brandy or cognac
- 1 tablespoon soy sauce
- Salt and freshly ground black pepper
- 1⁄2 cup raw cashews, soaked for 3 hours, then drained
- Chopped fresh parsley, for garnish

1. Heat the oil in a medium skillet over medium heat. Add the onion and garlic, cover, and cook until softened, about 5 minutes. Uncover and add the mushrooms and savory. Stir in the brandy, soy sauce, and salt and pepper to taste. Cook, stirring occasionally, until the mushrooms are soft and the liquid has evaporated, about 5 minutes. Let cool.

2. Place the cashews in a food processor and grind to a paste. Add the cooled mushroom mixture and process until smooth. Spoon the pâté into a small crock or serving bowl. Smooth the top and sprinkle with parsley. Cover and refrigerate for at least an hour before serving.

Soups, Stews, and Chilies

At once soothing, restorative, and satisfying, a steaming bowl of soup harkens back to the days when a pot of soup was a standard fixture on the stove. In today's convenience-oriented society, soup remains a favorite because it is a simple and inexpensive way to get healthy and delicious food on the table. Innovative and versatile, soups can be enjoyed as a first course, main dish, or even dessert.

Soup making is very forgiving. If it turns out too thick, add more water or broth. If too thin, cook uncovered to reduce the liquid, add more solids, or puree some of the existing solids. To avoid overseasoning, add the herbs and spices judiciously and check the seasonings near the end of cooking time.

Hearty Minestrone Soup

Greens and Beans Soup

Asparagus-Edamame Bisque

Mushroom Medley Soup

Black Bean Soup with a Splash

Curried Butternut and Red Lentil Soup with Chard

Thai-Inspired Coconut Soup

Spicy Pinto Bean and Tomato Soup with Green Chiles

Three-Alarm Chili

Chinese Black Bean Chili

Ratatouille

African-Inspired Red Bean Stew

Brazilian Black Bean Stew

Hearty Minestrone Soup

SERVES 4 TO 6

This classic Italian vegetable soup tastes better the day after it is made, so plan to make it ahead of time. Feel free to vary the vegetables as desired. For example, you can substitute spinach for the cabbage or use white beans or chickpeas in place of the kidney beans. Instead of barley, small cooked soup pasta makes a good addition, but for best results, the pasta should be cooked separately and added when ready to serve.

- 1 tablespoon olive oil
- 1 large yellow onion, minced
- 1 celery rib, chopped
- 1 large carrot, chopped
- 3 garlic cloves, minced
- 2 cups shredded cabbage
- 1 (14-ounce) can diced tomatoes, undrained
- 1½ cups cooked or 1 (15.5-ounce) can dark red kidney beans, drained and rinsed
- ¼ cup pearl barley
- ¼ cup dried split peas
- 6 cups vegetable broth or water
- ½ teaspoon dried oregano
- ½ teaspoon dried basil
- Salt and freshly ground black pepper
- 3 tablespoons chopped fresh parsley

1. Heat the oil in a large pot over medium heat. Add the onion, celery, carrot, and garlic. Cover and cook until softened, about 5 minutes. Stir in the cabbage, tomatoes, kidney beans, barley, and split peas. Add the broth, oregano, and basil and season with salt and pepper to taste. Bring to a boil, then decrease the heat to low and simmer, partially covered, for 1 hour or longer, until the vegetables are tender.

2. Taste and adjust the seasonings, if needed. Add a bit more broth if the liquid reduces too much. Just before serving, stir in the parsley.

Greens and Beans Soup

SERVES 4

This quick and delicious soup is a weekly regular at my house. I make it with whatever variety of greens (and beans) I have on hand. For a heartier soup, I like to add some cooked rice or pasta to the pot a few minutes before serving time.

1 tablespoon olive oil
1 large yellow onion, chopped
4 large garlic cloves, minced
3 cups cooked or 2 (15.5-ounce) cans cannellini beans
   or your favorite beans, drained and rinsed
6 cups vegetable broth
1 teaspoon dried basil
½ teaspoon dried oregano
¼ teaspoon red pepper flakes
   Salt and freshly ground black pepper
6 cups coarsely chopped kale or other dark leafy greens

1. Heat the oil in a large pot over medium heat. Add the onion, cover, and cook until softened, about 5 minutes. Add the garlic and cook for 1 minute longer.

2. Stir in the beans, broth, basil, oregano, red pepper flakes, and salt and pepper to taste. Bring to a boil, then decrease the heat to a simmer. Stir in the greens and continue to cook until the greens are tender and the flavors have melded, 15 to 20 minutes. Taste and adjust the seasonings, if needed. Serve hot.

Asparagus-Edamame Bisque

SERVES 4

For the creamiest texture, puree this elegant and delicious soup in a high-speed blender or, if using a regular blender or food processor, strain through a fine-mesh sieve before serving. As an optional garnish, you might reserve some cooked edamame or asparagus tips.

- 1 tablespoon olive oil
- 2 leeks, white part only, chopped
- 2 shallots, chopped
- 4 cups vegetable broth
- 1½ cups fresh or frozen shelled edamame, thawed if frozen
  Salt
- 1 pound fresh asparagus, trimmed and cut into 1-inch lengths
  Cayenne pepper
  Black sesame seeds or minced fresh parsley, for garnish (optional)

1. Heat the oil in a large pot over medium heat. Add the leeks and shallots, cover, and cook until softened, about 5 minutes. Add the broth, edamame, and salt to taste. Bring to a boil, then decrease the heat to low and simmer for 15 minutes. Add the asparagus and cayenne to taste. Return to a boil, then decrease the heat to medium, cover, and cook until the vegetables are tender, about 10 minutes longer.

2. Transfer the soup to a high-speed blender or food processor and puree until smooth. Return the soup to the pot; taste and adjust the seasonings, adding more liquid if too thick. Reheat the soup over low heat until hot. To serve, ladle into bowls and garnish with sesame seeds or parsley, if desired.

Mushroom Medley Soup

SERVES 4 TO 6

For more contrast and depth of flavor, include some morel, porcini, or oyster mushrooms, if available. Cooked rice, barley, or orzo, added near the end of the cooking time, makes a good addition. For some added color, you can also add ½ cup of frozen baby peas about 10 minutes prior to serving time.

  1 tablespoon olive oil
  1 large yellow onion, chopped
  1 carrot, chopped
  1 celery rib, chopped
  8 ounces shiitake mushrooms, stemmed and sliced
  8 ounces cremini mushrooms, sliced or quartered
  8 ounces white mushrooms, sliced
  6 cups vegetable broth
  ¼ cup chopped fresh parsley
  1 teaspoon minced fresh thyme, or ½ teaspoon dried
     Salt and freshly ground black pepper

Heat the oil in a large pot over medium heat. Add the onion, carrot, and celery. Cover and cook until softened, about 10 minutes. Stir in the mushrooms, add the broth, and bring to a boil. Decrease the heat to low, add the parsley and thyme, and season with salt and pepper to taste. Simmer until the vegetables are tender, about 30 minutes. Serve hot.

Black Bean Soup with a Splash

SERVES 4 TO 6

Sherry makes a good addition to this creamy black bean soup, but since not everyone at your table may agree, serve the sherry separately so diners can add their own splash at will. This can make for a fun presentation if you have an attractive cruet or shot glasses in which to serve the sherry.

  1 tablespoon olive oil
  2 carrots, chopped
  1 large yellow onion, chopped
  1 celery rib, chopped
  1 small green bell pepper, seeded and chopped
  2 garlic cloves, minced
  4 cups vegetable broth
4½ cups cooked or 3 (15.5-ounce) cans black beans, drained and rinsed
  1 teaspoon dried marjoram or thyme
  1 teaspoon salt
  ¼ teaspoon freshly ground black pepper
  2 tablespoons minced fresh parsley or cilantro
  ⅓ cup dry sherry

1. Heat the oil in a large pot over medium heat. Add the carrots, onion, celery, bell pepper, and garlic. Cover and cook until the vegetables are tender, stirring occasionally, about 10 minutes. Add the broth, beans, marjoram, salt, and pepper. Bring to a boil, then decrease the heat to low and simmer until the soup has thickened, about 45 minutes.

2. Use an immersion blender to puree some of the soup, or pulse a portion of the soup in a blender or food processor, then return the soup to the pot to reheat.

3. When ready to serve, ladle the soup into bowls and garnish with the parsley. Serve accompanied by the sherry, which you can pour into a cruet or individual shot glasses to be splashed into the soup at the table according to taste.

Curried Butternut and Red Lentil Soup with Chard

SERVES 4 TO 6

This fragrant soup has a rich complexity of flavor that tastes like it took hours to make. Serve it with warm roti, paratha, or other Indian bread. Substitute kale or spinach for the chard, if desired.

- 1 tablespoon olive oil
- 1 large yellow onion, chopped
- 1 small butternut squash, peeled and diced
- 1 garlic clove, minced
- 1 tablespoon minced fresh ginger
- 1 tablespoon curry powder
- 5 cups vegetable broth or water
- 1 (14.5-ounce) can crushed tomatoes
- 1 cup red lentils, picked over and rinsed
  Salt and freshly ground black pepper
- 3 cups chopped Swiss chard

1. Heat the oil in a large pot over medium heat. Add the onion, squash, and garlic. Cover and cook until softened, about 10 minutes. Stir in the ginger and curry powder, then add the broth, tomatoes, lentils, and salt and pepper to taste.

2. Bring to a boil, then decrease the heat to low and simmer until the lentils and vegetables are partly tender, stirring occasionally, about 15 minutes. Stir in the chard and simmer for 15 minutes longer, until everything is tender. Serve hot.

Thai-Inspired Coconut Soup

SERVES 4

This smooth and spicy soup has all the flavor you'd expect from a Thai-inspired soup, but without all the fuss—or exotic ingredients. Using ginger instead of galangal and lime juice instead of kaffir lime leaves, this soup is made with easy-to-find ingredients.

- 1 tablespoon grapeseed oil
- 1 large yellow onion, chopped
- 2 tablespoons soy sauce
- 1 tablespoon grated fresh ginger
- 2 teaspoons sugar
- 1 teaspoon Asian chili paste
- 2½ cups vegetable broth or water
- 8 ounces extra-firm tofu, cut into small dice
- 2 (13.5-ounce) cans unsweetened coconut milk
- 1 tablespoon fresh lime juice
- 3 tablespoons chopped fresh cilantro

1. Heat the oil in a large pot over medium heat. Add the onion and cook until softened, about 5 minutes. Stir in the soy sauce, ginger, sugar, and chili paste. Add the broth and bring to a boil. Decrease the heat to medium and simmer for 15 minutes.

2. Strain the onion and ginger out of the broth and discard. Return the broth to the pot over medium heat. Add the tofu and stir in the coconut milk and lime juice. Simmer for 5 minutes longer to allow the flavors to blend. Serve hot, sprinkled with the cilantro.

Spicy Pinto Bean and Tomato Soup with Green Chiles

SERVES 4

The surprising addition of peanut butter adds a mellow richness to this spicy soup. If you don't like the heat, use mild green chiles instead of hot ones—the soup will still be immensely flavorful.

- 1 tablespoon olive oil
- 1 large yellow onion, chopped
- 1 (28-ounce) can crushed tomatoes
- 1½ cups cooked or 1 (15.5-ounce) can pinto beans, drained and rinsed
- 1 (4-ounce) can diced hot or mild green chiles, drained
- 4 cups vegetable broth or water
- 2 tablespoons creamy peanut butter
  Salt
- 1 tablespoon fresh lime juice
  Minced fresh parsley or cilantro, for garnish

1. Heat the oil in a large pot over medium heat. Add the onion, cover, and cook until soft, about 10 minutes. Add the tomatoes, pinto beans, and chiles. Simmer, covered, for 15 minutes. Stir in the broth, peanut butter, and salt to taste and simmer for 15 minutes longer.

2. Use an immersion blender to puree the soup in the pot or transfer to a blender or food processor and puree until smooth, then return the soup to the pot. Stir in the lime juice and simmer, stirring, until hot. Serve garnished with parsley.

Three-Alarm Chili

SERVES 4

You can make this chili more or less "alarming" to suit your own heat tolerance. If you want more heat, use two chiles and a hot chili powder. For a milder version, omit the chiles, use a mild to medium chili powder, and add cayenne at your own discretion.

- 1 tablespoon olive oil
- 1 large yellow onion, chopped
- 1 small red bell pepper, seeded and chopped
- 1 or 2 jalapeño or serrano chiles, seeded and minced
- 4 garlic cloves, minced
- 1 (28-ounce) can crushed tomatoes
- 1½ cups water or vegetable broth
- 2 tablespoons chili powder
- ½ teaspoon dried oregano
- ½ teaspoon ground cumin
- ½ teaspoon smoked paprika
- ¼ teaspoon cayenne pepper
- ½ teaspoon salt
- ¼ teaspoon freshly ground black pepper
- 3 cups cooked or 2 (15.5-ounce) cans dark red kidney beans, drained and rinsed
- 1½ cups cooked or 1 (15.5-ounce) can pinto beans, drained and rinsed
- 1 cup frozen corn kernels, thawed (optional)

1. Heat the oil in a large saucepan over medium heat. Add the onion, bell pepper, chiles, and garlic. Cover and cook until softened, about 10 minutes.

2. Stir in the tomatoes, water, chili powder, oregano, cumin, paprika, cayenne, salt, and black pepper. Bring to a boil, then decrease the heat to low and stir in the beans. Cover and simmer for 20 minutes, stirring occasionally. Uncover; taste and adjust the seasonings, if needed (you may need to add more salt if you used water instead of broth). Simmer, uncovered, stirring occasionally, for about 15 minutes longer. A few minutes before you're ready to serve, stir in the corn, if using.

Chinese Black Bean Chili

SERVES 4

Garlicky black bean sauce adds a rich layer of flavor to this satisfying and unusual chili. Be aware that the black bean sauce is very salty, so be sure to taste for flavor before seasoning with salt. I like to serve this chili over rice.

- 1 tablespoon olive oil
- 1 yellow onion, chopped
- 1 carrot, chopped
- 2 tablespoons chili powder
- 1 teaspoon grated fresh ginger
- 1 teaspoon sugar
- 1 (28-ounce) can diced tomatoes, drained
- 1 cup water
- ½ cup Chinese black bean sauce
- 4½ cups cooked or 3 (15.5-ounce) cans black beans, drained and rinsed
  Salt and freshly ground black pepper
  Finely minced scallions, for garnish

1. Heat the oil in a large pot over medium heat. Add the onion and carrot. Cover and cook until softened, about 8 minutes. Stir in the chili powder, ginger, and sugar. Add the tomatoes, water, and black bean sauce.

2. Stir in the black beans and season with salt and pepper to taste. Bring to a boil, then decrease the heat to medium and simmer, covered, until the vegetables are tender, about 30 minutes. Simmer, uncovered, for about 10 minutes longer. Serve hot, garnished with scallions.

Ratatouille

SERVES 4 TO 6

The addition of white beans to this classic Provençal vegetable stew makes it hearty enough to enjoy as a one-dish meal served with warm, crusty bread.

- 1 tablespoon olive oil
- 1 yellow onion, chopped
- 3 garlic cloves, chopped
- 2 zucchini, chopped
- 1 eggplant, peeled and chopped
- 1 red bell pepper, seeded and chopped
- 1 yellow bell pepper, seeded and chopped
- 1 (14.5-ounce) can diced tomatoes, drained
- 1½ cups cooked or 1 (15.5-ounce) can white beans, drained and rinsed
  Salt and freshly ground black pepper
- ½ cup vegetable broth or water
- 1 teaspoon dried marjoram
- 1 teaspoon dried thyme
- 2 tablespoons chopped fresh parsley

1. Heat the oil in a large pot over medium heat. Add the onion, cover, and cook until softened, about 5 minutes. Add the garlic and cook for 30 seconds. Stir in the zucchini, eggplant, red and yellow bell peppers, tomatoes, and beans. Season with salt and black pepper to taste and cook, stirring, for 5 minutes. Add the broth, marjoram, and thyme. Cover, decrease the heat to low, and simmer until the vegetables are tender but not mushy, about 30 minutes.

2. Stir in the parsley; taste and adjust the seasonings, if needed. Serve warm.

African-Inspired Red Bean Stew

SERVES 4

Peanut butter is used to thicken and enrich this delectable stew studded with mahogany-colored kidney beans. Spoon it over a bed of rice, quinoa, or couscous to soak up every drop of the luscious sauce.

- 1 tablespoon olive oil
- 2 carrots, sliced
- 1 yellow onion, chopped
- 3 garlic cloves, minced
- 1 teaspoon grated fresh ginger
- 2 large Yukon Gold or russet potatoes, diced
- 3 cups cooked dark red kidney beans or 2 (15.5-ounce) cans, drained and rinsed
- 1 (14.5-ounce) can crushed tomatoes
- 1 (4-ounce) can diced mild green chiles, drained
- 1½ cups water or vegetable broth
- ½ teaspoon ground cumin
- ⅛ teaspoon cayenne pepper
- Salt and freshly ground black pepper
- ¼ cup peanut butter
- 3 cups baby spinach
- ⅓ cup chopped or crushed roasted peanuts

1. Heat the oil in a large pot over medium heat. Add the carrots and onion, cover, and cook until softened, about 10 minutes. Stir in the garlic and ginger. Cook until fragrant, about 1 minute.

2. Add the potatoes, kidney beans, tomatoes, chiles, 1 cup of the water, the cumin, and cayenne. Season with salt and pepper to taste. Cover and bring to a boil, then decrease the heat to low and simmer until the vegetables are soft, about 20 minutes.

3. In a small bowl, combine the peanut butter and the remaining ½ cup water, stirring until blended, then stir it into the stew. Add the spinach and cook, stirring, until wilted. Taste and adjust the seasonings, if needed. Serve hot, sprinkled with the peanuts.

Brazilian Black Bean Stew

SERVES 4

This tantalizing recipe was inspired by one shared with me by my friend Francis Janes, a talented vegan cook. Not only is this gorgeous stew visually appealing, but the flavor is sublime as well. Serve over freshly cooked quinoa or rice.

- 1 tablespoon olive oil
- 1 large red onion, chopped
- 3 garlic cloves, minced
- 1 medium sweet potato, peeled and diced
- 1 red bell pepper, seeded and diced
- 1 (14.5-ounce) can diced tomatoes, undrained
- 1 jalapeño chile, seeded and minced
- 1 cup vegetable broth
- 3 cups cooked or 2 (15.5-ounce) cans black beans, drained and rinsed
- ½ teaspoon salt
- 1 ripe mango, peeled, pitted, and diced
- ½ cup chopped fresh cilantro

1. Heat the oil in a large pot over medium heat. Add the onion, cover, and cook until softened, about 5 minutes, Stir in the garlic and cook for 2 minutes longer. Stir in the sweet potato, bell pepper, tomatoes, chile, and broth. Bring to a boil. Decrease the heat to low, cover, and simmer until the sweet potatoes are tender but still firm, about 15 minutes.

2. Stir in the beans and salt. Simmer gently, uncovered, until heated through, about 5 minutes. Stir in the mango and cook until heated through, about 1 minute. Stir in the cilantro and serve hot.

Lunch and Brunch Bunch

Even though many of us eat the same thing each day for breakfast, no collection of "best" recipes is complete without a few go-to recipes for lunch or brunch. What makes these "best" recipes even better is the fact that they also make great dinners! And with dazzling flavor combos like Spinach and Mushroom Black Bean Quesadillas (page 68) and Bánh Mì Tostadas (page 61), you'll never get bored.

Sunday Frittata

Bánh Mì Tostadas

White Bean and Potato-Mushroom Burritos

Provençal Burgers

Couscous Brunch Cake with Peaches and Blueberries

Spinach and Mushroom Black Bean Quesadillas

Sloppy Bulgur Sandwiches

Portobello Po'boys

Falafel Sandwiches

Sunday Frittata

SERVES 4

I call this Sunday Frittata because that's the day of the week when I like to make it for brunch. I usually add whatever vegetables I have on hand—it's an especially good way to use up leftover cooked vegetables, if you have any.

- 1 tablespoon olive oil
- 1 small yellow onion, minced
- 3 garlic cloves, minced
- 1 cup chopped mushrooms (any kind)
- 3 cups chopped kale, spinach, or Swiss chard
  Salt and freshly ground black pepper
- 1 pound firm tofu, well drained
- ¼ cup nutritional yeast
- 3 tablespoons minced oil-packed or reconstituted sun-dried tomatoes
- 1 tablespoon fresh lemon juice
- ½ teaspoon dried basil
- ½ teaspoon dried oregano
- ½ teaspoon smoked paprika
  Pinch of ground turmeric
- ⅓ cup shredded vegan cheese (optional)

1. Preheat the oven to 375°F. Lightly oil a 9-inch pie pan, cake pan, or springform pan.

2. Heat the oil in a large skillet over medium heat. Add the onion and cook until softened, 5 minutes. Add the garlic and mushrooms, and cook, stirring occasionally, for 4 minutes longer. Add the kale and continue to cook, stirring, until the greens are wilted, about 5 minutes longer. Season with salt and pepper to taste and set aside.

3. Press or squeeze any remaining liquid out of the tofu and crumble into a large bowl. Add the nutritional yeast, tomatoes, lemon juice, basil, oregano, paprika, turmeric, ½ teaspoon salt, and ¼ teaspoon pepper. Use your hands or a potato ricer to mix and mash well.

4. Drain any liquid off the reserved vegetables and add them to the tofu mixture, along with the vegan cheese, if using. Mix well. Taste and adjust the seasonings, if needed.

5. Spread the mixture evenly in the prepared pan, pressing well. Bake until firm and golden brown, about 40 minutes. Cut into wedges and serve hot.

Bánh Mì Tostadas

SERVES 4 TO 6

East meets West in this tasty fusion combo. Tostada means "toasted" in Spanish and is the name of a Mexican dish in which a toasted tortilla is the base for other ingredients that top it. Bánh mì is a popular Vietnamese sandwich that features crisp pickled vegetables, fragrant cilantro, chiles, and zesty hoisin and sriracha sauces. In this iteration, bánh mì ingredients find themselves on toasted tortillas instead of in a baguette to make Bánh Mì Tostadas. Corn tortillas are usually used for tostadas, although wheat tortillas may be used if you prefer.

TOPPINGS:

- 1 large carrot, shredded
- ½ English cucumber, peeled, seeded, and chopped
- 2 cups finely shredded cabbage
- 1 cup fresh cilantro leaves
- 1 to 2 tablespoons chopped pickled jalapeño chiles (optional)
- 1 teaspoon dark (toasted) sesame oil
- 1 tablespoon neutral vegetable oil
- 2 garlic cloves, minced
- ¼ cup minced scallions
- 1½ teaspoons grated fresh ginger
- 1 (8-ounce) package baked tofu, cut into thin strips
- 3 tablespoons soy sauce
- 3 tablespoons hoisin sauce
- 2 tablespoons rice vinegar
- 1 to 2 teaspoons sriracha sauce
- 1 teaspoon sugar

TOSTADA SHELLS:

- 4 to 6 corn or flour tortillas
- 2 tablespoons grapeseed oil

Toppings:

1. In a large bowl, combine the carrot, cucumber, cabbage, cilantro, and jalapeños, if using. Drizzle on the sesame oil and toss gently to combine. Set aside.

CONTINUED ON PAGE 62

CONTINUED FROM PAGE 61

2. Heat the vegetable oil in a skillet over medium heat. Add the garlic, scallions, and ginger and cook for 1 minute. Add the tofu and 1 tablespoon of the soy sauce and mix well to coat the tofu. Set aside to cool.

3. In a small bowl, combine the remaining 2 tablespoons soy sauce, the hoisin, vinegar, sriracha, and sugar, stirring well to blend.

Tostada shells:

4. Preheat the oven to 400°F. Arrange the tortillas in a single layer on two baking sheets. Brush both sides of each tortilla with oil. Bake for 5 minutes on one side, then flip the tortillas over and bake for 2 to 3 minutes longer, until crispy. Watch carefully so they don't burn.

To assemble:

5. Evenly divide the tofu among the tostada shells. Top each with some of the vegetable mixture, then the sauce. Serve immediately.

White Bean and Potato-Mushroom Burritos

SERVES 4

This is a great way to use up leftover baked potatoes (or make some extra to use for this). Add some chopped spinach, kale, or chard, if desired, when you add the mushrooms.

- 1 tablespoon olive oil
- 1 small yellow onion, minced
- 3 garlic cloves, minced
- 4 ounces chopped mushrooms (any kind)
- 2 cups diced cooked potato
- ½ cup tomato salsa, plus more for serving
- 1 teaspoon chili powder
- ½ teaspoon salt
- ¼ teaspoon freshly ground black pepper
- 1 (15.5-ounce) can cannellini or other white beans, drained, rinsed, and mashed
- ½ cup shredded vegan cheese (optional)
- 4 (10-inch) flour tortillas, warmed

1. Heat the oil in a saucepan over medium heat. Add the onion and cook until softened, 5 minutes. Add the garlic and mushrooms and cook for 3 minutes longer, or until softened. Add the cooked potato, salsa, chili powder, salt, and pepper. Stir in the mashed beans and cheese, if using. Cook, stirring occasionally, until hot. Taste and adjust the seasonings, if needed.

2. To serve, divide the bean mixture evenly among the tortillas, spread it down the center of each. Add more salsa, if you like, and roll up the tortillas, tucking in the sides as you roll. Serve immediately, or place the filled burritos (one at a time) in a hot nonstick skillet for a minute or two—just long enough to lightly brown the outside of the tortillas.

Provençal Burgers

SERVES 4

Studded with olives, sun-dried tomatoes, and roasted red bell peppers, these flavor-packed burgers are bursting with the taste of Provence. They are especially delicious served on lightly toasted ciabatta rolls.

- 1 (15.5-ounce) can chickpeas, drained, rinsed, and blotted dry
- ½ cup minced scallions
- ¼ cup chopped roasted red bell peppers, blotted dry
- ¼ cup chopped oil-packed or reconstituted sun-dried tomatoes, blotted dry
- 2 tablespoons pitted Kalamata olives, blotted dry
- 1 cup old-fashioned rolled oats
- 1 tablespoon arrowroot or cornstarch
- 1 teaspoon salt
- ½ teaspoon garlic powder
- ¼ teaspoon freshly ground black pepper
  Dried bread crumbs, if needed
- 2 tablespoons olive oil, plus more if needed

TO SERVE:
- ¼ cup vegan mayonnaise
- 2 tablespoons tapenade (optional)
- 4 ciabatta rolls or burger buns, toasted
- 4 lettuce leaves
- 4 tomato slices

1. In a food processor, combine the chickpeas, scallions, roasted red bell pepper, tomatoes, olives, and oats. Pulse to break up and mix, but do not puree. Transfer the mixture to a bowl. Add the arrowroot, salt, garlic powder, and black pepper. Mix well to combine. If the mixture is too wet, add some bread crumbs, ¼ cup at a time. If the mixture is too dry, add a little olive oil, 1 tablespoon at a time.

2. Divide the mixture into four equal portions. Shape each portion into patties, ½ inch thick. Refrigerate or freeze the burgers for 15 minutes to firm up.

3. Heat the oil in a large skillet over medium heat. Add the burgers and cook until well browned, about 3 minutes per side, adding a little more oil if needed.

4. To serve, spread the mayo and tapenade, if using, on the bottom of each toasted roll. Top with a lettuce leaf and a tomato slice, then arrange a burger on top and serve immediately.

Baked Variation:

Preheat the oven to 375°F. Arrange the burgers on a baking sheet lined with parchment paper and bake for about 15 minutes per side.

Couscous Brunch Cake with Peaches and Blueberries

SERVES 6

This is one of my favorite brunch dishes, especially when serving a crowd. It is delicious and satisfying. Best of all, it can be made ahead of time and it looks beautiful with fresh fruit cascading down around it. If you're putting it on the table whole rather than plating it, you can cut it and then top it with the fruit for easier serving.

    2 cups white grape juice
    1 cup couscous
    1 tablespoon granulated sugar
    ½ teaspoon ground cinnamon
    1 cup fresh blueberries
    2 peaches, pitted and chopped
    2 teaspoons superfine sugar
    1 teaspoon fresh lemon juice

1. Lightly oil a 9-inch springform pan. Bring the juice to a boil in a saucepan. Add the couscous, granulated sugar, and cinnamon. Decrease the heat to low, cover, and simmer until the juice has been absorbed, about 5 minutes. Press the mixture into the springform pan. Cover loosely and refrigerate for at least an hour.

2. In a bowl, combine the blueberries, peaches, superfine sugar, and lemon juice. Stir to mix well. Set aside at room temperature for 30 minutes. To serve, cut the cake into wedges and top each slice with some of the fruit.

Spinach and Mushroom Black Bean Quesadillas

SERVES 4

Including tender, fresh baby spinach in the quesadilla filling is a fun way to get kids to eat their greens. And if you still can't win them over, that means more quesadillas for you.

1½ cups cooked or 1 (15.5-ounce) can black beans, drained and rinsed
1 tablespoon olive oil
½ cup minced red onion
2 garlic cloves, minced
2 cups sliced mushrooms (any kind)
4 cups baby spinach
   Salt and freshly ground black pepper
4 large flour tortillas

1. Place the black beans in a bowl and mash them with a potato ricer. Heat the oil in a small skillet over medium heat. Add the onion and garlic. Cover and cook until softened, about 5 minutes. Stir in the mushrooms and cook until softened. Add the spinach, season with salt and pepper to taste, and cook, stirring, until the spinach is wilted. Uncover, stir in the black beans, and cook, stirring, until the liquid has been absorbed.

2. Divide the mixture among the tortillas, spreading it evenly over the bottom half of each tortilla. Fold the top half of the tortillas over the filling, pressing down lightly to hold them together. Place two of the quesadillas in a large nonstick skillet or griddle over medium heat. Cook until lightly browned on both sides, turning once. Repeat with the remaining quesadillas. To serve, cut the quesadillas into three or four wedges each and arrange on plates.

Sloppy Bulgur Sandwiches

SERVES 4

A meatless sloppy joe can be made with crumbled tempeh or tofu, lentils, TVP (textured vegetable protein), or frozen veggie burger crumbles. All work well when simmered in the zesty tomato sauce we know and love. In this version, the use of bulgur, a tender, chewy grain, ensures that these sloppy sandwiches are not your average joes.

- 1 cup bulgur
- Salt
- 1 tablespoon olive oil
- 1 small red onion, minced
- ½ red bell pepper, seeded and minced
- 1 (14.5-ounce) can crushed tomatoes
- 1 tablespoon sugar
- 1 tablespoon mustard
- 2 teaspoons soy sauce
- 1 teaspoon chili powder
- Freshly ground black pepper
- 4 sandwich rolls

1. Combine the bulgur with 1¾ cups water in a saucepan. Bring to a boil, then decrease the heat to low and add salt to taste. Cover and cook until the bulgur is tender and the water has been absorbed, about 15 minutes.

2. While the bulgur is simmering, heat the oil in a large skillet over medium heat. Add the onion and bell pepper, cover, and cook until soft, about 7 minutes. Stir in the tomatoes, sugar, mustard, soy sauce, chili powder, and salt and pepper to taste. Simmer for 10 minutes, stirring frequently. To serve, spoon the bulgur mixture onto the rolls.

Portobello Po'boys

SERVES 4

Juicy chunks of portobello mushrooms replace the traditional oysters in this flavorful interpretation of the Southern classic. Leave the Tabasco bottle on the table for anyone who wants an extra splash.

- 3 tablespoons olive oil
- 4 portobello mushroom caps, cut into 1- to 2-inch pieces
- 1/2 teaspoon Cajun seasoning blend
  Salt and freshly ground black pepper
- 4 crusty sandwich rolls
  Vegan mayonnaise, for spreading
- 4 tomato slices
- 1 1/2 cups shredded romaine lettuce
  Tabasco sauce, for serving

1. Heat the oil in a large skillet over medium heat. Add the mushroom pieces and cook until browned and softened, about 8 minutes. Add the Cajun seasoning blend and salt and pepper to taste.

2. Spread the rolls with mayonnaise. Place a tomato slice on the bottom of each roll, and top each with some of the shredded lettuce. Arrange the mushroom pieces on top, sprinkle with Tabasco, and top with the roll tops.

Falafel Sandwiches

SERVES 4 TO 6

Falafel is the fast-food burger of Middle Eastern cuisines. Made with chickpeas and fragrantly spiced, these sturdy patties are especially delicious stuffed into pitas and served with Lemon-Tahini Sauce.

1½ cups cooked or 1 (15.5-ounce) can chickpeas, drained, rinsed, and blotted dry
1 cup old-fashioned rolled oats
1 small onion, chopped
3 garlic cloves, chopped
3 tablespoons chopped fresh parsley
1 teaspoon ground cumin
1 teaspoon ground coriander
¾ teaspoon salt
¼ teaspoon freshly ground black pepper
    Chickpea flour or all-purpose flour, as needed
    Olive oil
4 to 6 loaves pita bread
    Shredded lettuce, for serving
    Sliced tomato, for serving
    Lemon-Tahini Sauce (recipe follows), for serving

1. In a food processor, combine the chickpeas, oats, onion, garlic, parsley, cumin, coriander, salt, and pepper and process to combine. Refrigerate for 30 minutes or longer.

2. Form the mixture into small balls, about 2 inches in diameter. If the mixture is not firm enough, add up to ⅓ cup flour, a little at a time, until the desired consistency is reached. Flatten the balls into patties and dredge them in flour. Heat a layer of oil in a large skillet over medium-high heat. Add the falafel and cook, turning once, until golden brown, about 8 minutes total. To serve, stuff the falafel patties into the pita bread along with lettuce, tomato slices, and tahini sauce.

Lemon-Tahini Sauce

MAKES ABOUT ½ CUP

In addition to serving this creamy tahini sauce on the Falafel Sandwiches, spoon it over baked marinated tofu or drizzled over kale, spinach, or rice and beans—it's sensational. You can also double the recipe and toss it with noodles.

- 3 tablespoons tahini (sesame paste)
- 2 tablespoons fresh lemon juice
- 2 tablespoons soy sauce
- 1 teaspoon minced garlic
- 1 tablespoon dark (toasted) sesame oil
- 1 tablespoon minced fresh parsley
- 1 to 2 tablespoons water (optional)

In a bowl, combine the tahini, lemon juice, soy sauce, and garlic. Whisk together to blend. Whisk in the sesame oil, blending well. Stir in the parsley, and add a little water if you prefer a thinner sauce.

Special Salads

No iceberg wedges or bottled dressing allowed! This chapter features sensational salads made with a variety of textures and flavors, from Pasta Salad with Grilled Summer Vegetables (page 83) to Mexican Black Bean and Corn Salad with Cilantro Dressing (page 82). This chapter has salads for every taste, from the luxurious Watercress, Fennel, and Avocado Salad with Dried Cherries and Macadamias (page 78) to the not-your-average slaw: Carrot Super-Slaw with Edamame and Almonds (page 76).

Carrot Super-Slaw with Edamame and Almonds

Chilled Glass Noodles with Snow Peas and Baked Tofu

Watercress, Fennel, and Avocado Salad with
    Dried Cherries and Macadamias

Autumn Harvest Salad

West Coast Greek Salad

Mexican Black Bean and Corn Salad with
    Cilantro Dressing

Pasta Salad with Grilled Summer Vegetables

Chickpea "Tuna" Salad in Avocados

Roasted Potato Salad with Chickpeas,
    Sun-Dried Tomatoes, and Peas

Carrot Super-Slaw with Edamame and Almonds

SERVES 4

This slaw is super for a lot of reasons, from the crisp and colorful shredded carrots and protein-rich edamame to the creamy, sweet, and tangy dressing and the crunch of toasted almonds. Add to that the fact that it's also delicious and healthful, and you've got one super slaw.

- 3 tablespoons fresh lime juice
- 2 tablespoons almond butter
- 2 tablespoons mango or lime jam
- 2 tablespoons water
- 1 teaspoon salt
- 1 pound carrots, peeled and shredded
- 2 cups cooked shelled edamame
- ½ cup chopped fresh cilantro
- ¼ cup minced scallions
- ¼ cup slivered almonds, toasted

1. In a blender, combine the lime juice, almond butter, jam, water, and salt. Blend until smooth.

2. In a large bowl, combine the carrots, edamame, cilantro, and scallions. Add the dressing and toss to combine. Garnish with the almonds and serve.

Chilled Glass Noodles with Snow Peas and Baked Tofu

SERVES 4

Prepare this light but satisfying salad at least 30 minutes ahead of time for the best flavor. Made from mung bean flour, glass noodles are also called cellophane noodles, bean thread noodles, and *harusame*. Marinated baked tofu is available at well-stocked supermarkets and natural foods stores. Look for one marinated with Thai or Asian flavors for best results.

- 4 ounces glass noodles
- 1 (8-ounce) package marinated baked tofu, cut into ½-inch dice
- 4 ounces snow peas, trimmed and diagonally cut into 1-inch pieces
- 1 English cucumber, peeled, seeded, and thinly sliced
- 1 carrot, grated
- ¼ cup minced scallions
- 2 tablespoons chopped fresh cilantro
- ½ cup unsalted roasted peanuts, crushed or chopped
- 3 tablespoons dark (toasted) sesame oil
- 2 tablespoons fresh lime juice
- 2 tablespoons rice vinegar
- 1 tablespoon soy sauce
- 1 garlic clove, minced
- 1 teaspoon sugar

1. Bring a saucepan of water to a boil. Add the noodles and remove from the heat. Let the noodles soak in the hot water until soft, 8 to 10 minutes. Drain well and rinse under cold water. Cut the noodles into thirds and place them in a large bowl. Add the tofu, snow peas, cucumber, carrot, scallions, cilantro, and peanuts.

2. In a small bowl, combine the sesame oil, lime juice, vinegar, soy sauce, garlic, and sugar, stirring to blend well. Add the dressing to the salad and toss gently to combine. Refrigerate for at least 30 minutes before serving.

Watercress, Fennel, and Avocado Salad with Dried Cherries and Macadamias

SERVES 4

This elegant salad, with its luxe ingredients, makes a great first course for a special dinner. Since dried cherries can be pricey, you might want to use the more economical dried cranberries. A different type of nut, such as walnuts or cashews, may be substituted for the macadamias as well. If watercress is unavailable, use more of your favorite salad greens.

- 3 tablespoons olive oil
- 2 tablespoons sherry vinegar
- 2 teaspoons chopped shallot
- 1/2 teaspoon sugar
- 1/2 teaspoon salt
- 1/8 teaspoon freshly ground black pepper
- 2 bunches watercress, tough stems removed (about 4 cups)
- 2 cups chopped salad greens
- 1 fennel bulb, thinly sliced
- 1/3 cup dried cherries or cranberries
- 1/4 cup macadamia nuts, coarsely chopped
- 1 ripe Hass avocado

1. In a food processor or blender, combine the oil, vinegar, shallot, sugar, salt, and pepper and blend until smooth.

2. In a large bowl, combine the watercress, salad greens, fennel, cherries, and macadamias. Pit and peel the avocado and cut into small dice. Add to the salad, along with the dressing, and toss gently to combine. Divide among salad plates to serve.

Autumn Harvest Salad

SERVES 4

The colors of autumn leaves and the vibrant produce of autumn were the inspiration for this beautiful salad. For a dramatic presentation, serve it on a bed of shredded red cabbage and romaine lettuce, tossed with a little additional dressing.

- 1½ pounds sweet potatoes, peeled and cut into ½-inch dice
- 2 tablespoons cider vinegar
- 1 tablespoon pure maple syrup
- ½ teaspoon Dijon mustard
- ½ teaspoon salt
- ⅛ teaspoon freshly ground black pepper
- ¼ cup grapeseed oil
- 1 Bosc pear
- 1 crisp red apple
- ½ cup chopped celery
- ½ cup walnuts or pecans, toasted
- ¼ cup sweetened dried cranberries
- 2 scallions, minced

1. Bring a pot of salted water to a boil and cook the sweet potatoes until just tender, about 20 minutes. Drain well, place in a large bowl, and set aside.

2. In a medium bowl, combine the vinegar, maple syrup, mustard, salt, and pepper. Whisk in the oil until blended.

3. Core the pear and apple, leaving the skin on, then cut them into ½-inch dice and add them to the bowl with the dressing, tossing to coat. Add the pear and apple mixture to the sweet potatoes. Add the celery, walnuts, cranberries, and scallions and toss gently to combine.

West Coast Greek Salad

SERVES 4

Tofu stands in for feta in this vegan version of a Greek salad, but the real star here is the creamy avocado. I like to serve this salad with warm grilled bread.

- 14 ounces extra-firm tofu, drained, rinsed, and blotted dry
- ¼ cup olive oil
- 2 tablespoons rice vinegar
- 1 tablespoon fresh lemon juice
- 1 garlic clove, minced
- ¾ teaspoon salt
- ½ teaspoon dried oregano
- ½ teaspoon dried basil
- ¼ teaspoon freshly ground black pepper
- 1 large head romaine lettuce, torn into bite-size pieces
- 1½ cups cooked or 1 (15.5-ounce) can chickpeas, drained and rinsed
- 1 English cucumber, peeled, seeded, and chopped
- ½ cup pitted Kalamata olives, halved
- ¼ cup pine nuts, toasted
- ¼ cup chopped fresh parsley
- 2 tablespoons minced scallions
- 2 ripe Hass avocados

1. Cut the tofu into ½-inch cubes and arrange in a shallow bowl or baking dish. In a bowl, combine the oil, vinegar, lemon juice, garlic, salt, oregano, basil, and pepper. Mix well and pour over the tofu. Marinate the tofu for at least 1 hour, tossing occasionally. If marinating longer than 1 hour, cover and refrigerate.

2. In a large bowl, combine the lettuce, chickpeas, cucumber, olives, pine nuts, parsley, and scallions. Pit, peel, and dice the avocados and add them to the salad. Add the tofu and marinade and toss gently to combine. Serve immediately.

Mexican Black Bean and Corn Salad with Cilantro Dressing

SERVES 4 TO 6

This attractive salad contains all the classic flavors of Mexican and Southwestern cuisine. Serve it on a bed of lettuce or cold cooked rice—or both.

- 3 cups cooked or 2 (15.5-ounce) cans black beans, drained and rinsed
- 2 cups frozen corn kernels, thawed
- ½ cup finely chopped red bell pepper
- 1 jalapeño chile, seeded and minced
- 2 tablespoons minced scallions
- 2 garlic cloves, crushed
- ¼ cup chopped fresh cilantro
- 1 teaspoon ground cumin
- ¾ teaspoon salt
- ¼ teaspoon freshly ground black pepper
- ¼ cup olive oil
- 2 tablespoons fresh lime juice
- 2 tablespoons water

1. In a large bowl, combine the beans, corn, bell pepper, jalapeño, and scallions.

2. In a blender or food processor, mince the garlic. Add the cilantro, cumin, salt, and black pepper and pulse to blend. Add the oil, lime juice, and water and process until well blended. Pour the dressing onto the salad and toss to combine. Taste and adjust the seasonings, if needed.

Pasta Salad with Grilled Summer Vegetables

SERVES 4

Add chickpeas or diced baked tofu for a more substantial salad. If a grill basket is unavailable, grill the vegetables whole or halved and cut them into bite-size pieces after they are cooked.

- 8 ounces radiatore or other small pasta
- 1/3 cup plus 2 tablespoons olive oil
- 3 tablespoons cider vinegar
- 1/2 teaspoon sugar
- 1/2 teaspoon salt
- 1/4 teaspoon dry mustard
- 1/8 teaspoon freshly ground black pepper
- 1 cup halved cherry tomatoes
- 1/4 cup chopped fresh parsley or basil
- 1 small zucchini, cut into 1/4-inch slices
- 1 small yellow squash, cut into 1/4-inch slices
- 1 red bell pepper, seeded and diced
- 1 red onion, diced
- 1 cup white mushrooms, quartered or sliced

1. Preheat the grill and lightly oil a grill basket. Bring a pot of salted water to a boil and cook the pasta until it is al dente, about 10 minutes. Drain well and transfer to a large bowl.

2. In a small bowl, combine the 1/3 cup oil, vinegar, sugar, salt, dry mustard, and black pepper. Pour enough of the dressing onto the pasta to coat. Add the cherry tomatoes and parsley and toss to combine.

3. In a separate bowl, combine the zucchini, yellow squash, bell pepper, onion, and mushrooms. Add the remaining 2 tablespoons oil and season with salt and black pepper. Toss to coat. Transfer the vegetables to the grill basket. Place the grill basket onto the hot grill and cook until the vegetables are grilled on the outside and slightly tender on the inside, 12 to 15 minutes. Add the grilled vegetables to the pasta mixture and toss to combine.

Chickpea "Tuna" Salad in Avocados

SERVES 2 TO 4

Chopped chickpeas supply the texture and kelp powder provides the taste of the sea for a salad reminiscent of tuna that looks and tastes great, especially when mounded onto avocado halves. Serve one or two avocado halves per person, depending on whether the salad is a first course or a main dish for a light lunch. Look for kelp powder (or nori or dulse flakes) in natural foods stores or, if you don't care about that taste of the sea, leave it out. This salad can also be served on a bed of lettuce, with the avocado diced and added on top.

1½ cups cooked or 1 (15.5-ounce) can chickpeas, drained and rinsed
½ cup finely minced celery
¼ cup minced red bell pepper
2 scallions, finely minced
⅓ cup vegan mayonnaise, plus more if needed
1 tablespoon plus 1 teaspoon fresh lemon juice
1 teaspoon Dijon mustard
1 teaspoon kelp powder (or nori or dulse flakes)
Salt and freshly ground black pepper
2 ripe Hass avocados
Lettuce leaves, for serving

1. In a food processor, pulse the chickpeas until coarsely chopped, then transfer to a large bowl. Add the celery, bell pepper, scallions, mayonnaise, 1 tablespoon of the lemon juice, the mustard, kelp powder, and salt and black pepper to taste. Mix well, adding a little more mayonnaise if the mixture seems dry. Cover and refrigerate for at least 30 minutes before serving.

2. When ready to serve, halve and pit the avocados and brush the exposed flesh with the remaining 1 teaspoon lemon juice to prevent discoloration. Divide the chickpea mixture among the avocado halves, pressing gently with a spoon to mound the salad onto the avocados. To serve, line salad plates with lettuce leaves and arrange the filled avocados on top.

Roasted Potato Salad with Chickpeas, Sun-Dried Tomatoes, and Peas

SERVES 4 TO 6

Roasting gives the potatoes loads of extra flavor in this hearty salad that is filling enough to serve as a main dish, thanks to the addition of protein-rich chickpeas.

1½ pounds small new potatoes, halved or quartered
¼ cup plus 1 tablespoon olive oil
    Salt and freshly ground black pepper
2 tablespoons white wine vinegar
1½ cups cooked or 1 (15.5-ounce) can chickpeas, drained and rinsed
¼ cup chopped oil-packed or reconstituted sun-dried tomatoes
1 cup frozen baby peas, thawed
1 shallot, halved lengthwise and thinly sliced
¼ cup chopped fresh parsley

1. Preheat the oven to 425°F. Place the potatoes in a bowl with 1 tablespoon of the olive oil. Season with salt and pepper to taste and toss to coat. Transfer the potatoes to a baking sheet and bake, turning once, until tender and golden brown, about 30 minutes. Let cool.

2. In a small bowl, combine the remaining ¼ cup oil with the vinegar and salt and pepper to taste. Place the cooled potatoes in a bowl along with the chickpeas, tomatoes, peas, shallot, and parsley. Pour on the dressing and toss gently to combine. Taste and adjust the seasonings, if needed. Serve warm or at room temperature.

Bean and Grain Mains

Whole grains and beans are mainstays of a healthy vegan diet, so they should make regular appearances on your menus. But just because you eat them frequently doesn't mean you need to eat them the same way every time. With delicious recipes such as Chimichurri White Beans and Roasted Asparagus (page 92), Piccata-Style Cashew-Chickpea Medallions (page 103), and Squash Stuffed with Black Beans, Rice, and Mango (page 91), a variety of savory options are at your fingertips.

Spinach, White Bean, and Pine Nut Strudel

SERVES 4 TO 6

Tender baby spinach is delicious, good for you, and easy to use. It combines creamy white beans and crunchy pine nuts in flaky pastry for a strudel vaguely reminiscent of spanakopita. Since pine nuts can be a bit pricey, walnuts can be used instead if you want to economize.

   2   tablespoons olive oil
   3   shallots, minced
   2   garlic cloves, minced
   6   cups baby spinach
1½   cups cooked or 1 (15.5-ounce) can white beans, drained and rinsed
   1   tablespoon fresh lemon juice
   ¾   teaspoon salt
   ½   teaspoon dried oregano
   ¼   teaspoon freshly ground black pepper
   ½   cup chopped pine nuts or walnuts
   1   sheet frozen puff pastry, thawed

1. Heat the oil in a large skillet over medium heat. Add the shallots and garlic, cover, and cook until softened, 3 minutes. Add the spinach and cook, stirring, until the spinach is wilted and any liquid has evaporated, about 4 minutes.

2. Place the beans in a bowl and mash them well. Add the spinach mixture, the lemon juice, salt, oregano, and pepper, stirring to mix well. Refrigerate to cool completely.

3. Preheat the oven to 425°F. Line a baking sheet with parchment paper. Roll out the thawed puff pastry and sprinkle with about one-third of the pine nuts. Spread the cooled spinach and bean mixture evenly across the dough and sprinkle with half of the remaining pine nuts. Fold over the sides and then roll the pastry up like a strudel. Place the strudel on the baking sheet, seam side down. Sprinkle with the remaining pine nuts. Bake until golden brown, 25 to 30 minutes.

Squash Stuffed with Black Beans, Rice, and Mango

SERVES 4

The vivid color contrasts and delectable flavors set this stuffed squash apart. If you can find the super-sweet brilliantly orange-fleshed kabocha squash, please buy it—it's the best-tasting squash on the planet. If you can't find a squash with a large cavity, use two smaller squashes.

- 1 large sweet winter squash, halved and seeded
- Salt
- 1 cup long-grain brown rice
- 1 tablespoon olive oil
- 6 scallions, minced
- 1 tablespoon grated fresh ginger
- 1 small hot or mild chile, seeded and minced
- 1½ cups cooked or 1 (15.5-ounce) can black beans, drained and rinsed
- 1 ripe mango, peeled, pitted, and chopped
- 2 teaspoons fresh lemon juice
- 2 teaspoons sugar
- ¼ cup minced fresh parsley
- Freshly ground black pepper

1. Preheat the oven to 375°F. Lightly oil a shallow baking pan. Season the squash halves with salt and place them in the baking pan, cut side down. Add ¼ inch water to the pan and cover tightly. Bake for 20 minutes to soften slightly.

2. Bring 2 cups salted water to a boil and add the rice. Decrease the heat to low, cover, and simmer until tender, about 40 minutes.

3. Heat the oil in a large skillet over medium heat. Add the scallions, ginger, and chile and cook until softened, about 3 minutes. Transfer to a large bowl. Add the cooked rice, beans, mango, lemon juice, sugar, and parsley and season with salt and pepper to taste. Mix thoroughly to combine well, then taste and adjust the seasonings, if needed. Turn the squash halves over, cut side up, and fill the squash cavities with the stuffing, packing well. Cover and bake until the stuffing is hot and the squash is tender, about 45 minutes.

Chimichurri White Beans and Roasted Asparagus

SERVES 4

This flavorful bean-asparagus combo is seasoned with a zesty Brazilian chimichurri sauce, made with lots of garlic and parsley. It's delicious over rice or quinoa or tossed with hot cooked pasta.

- 1 pound thin asparagus, trimmed and cut into 1-inch pieces
- 4 tablespoons olive oil
  Salt and freshly ground black pepper
- 4 cloves garlic, crushed
- 1 cup coarsely chopped fresh parsley
- 1½ teaspoons fresh oregano, or ½ teaspoon dried
- ¼ teaspoon red pepper flakes
  Pinch of sugar
- 1½ tablespoons rice vinegar
- 1½ cups cooked white beans or 1 (15.5-ounce) can white beans, drained and rinsed
- ¼ cup water

1. Preheat the oven to 425°F. In a bowl, combine the asparagus and 1 tablespoon of the oil. Season with salt and pepper to taste and toss to coat. Spread the asparagus on a baking pan and roast until tender, about 8 minutes.

2. In a small food processor, combine the garlic, parsley, oregano, red pepper flakes, ¼ teaspoon salt, ¼ teaspoon black pepper, and the sugar. Process to a paste. Add the vinegar and the remaining 3 tablespoons oil. Process until smooth.

3. In a saucepan, combine the beans and ¼ cup water. Cook, stirring, over medium heat until hot. When the asparagus is roasted, transfer it to the saucepan with the beans. Add the sauce and mix gently to combine. Serve hot.

Broccoli-Quinoa Mac

SERVES 4 TO 6

Like mac and cheese but made with quinoa, this dish is
bursting with flavor and nutrition. The creamy sauce
is made with cashews, white beans, and roasted red bell
pepper and seasoned with sherry, mustard, and nutritional
yeast. It's hard to believe a dish so comforting and
delicious is also so good for you.

1½ cups quinoa

2½ cups small broccoli florets

5 scallions, chopped

1½ cups raw cashews, soaked for 4 hours, then drained

1 cup cooked white beans

¼ cup chopped roasted red bell pepper

¼ cup nutritional yeast

2 tablespoons dry sherry

1 tablespoon cider vinegar

1 teaspoon Dijon mustard

1 teaspoon salt

½ teaspoon smoked paprika

1 cup plain unsweetened almond milk

¼ cup panko bread crumbs

1. Preheat the oven to 350°F. Lightly oil a baking dish.

2. Cook the quinoa according to the package directions. About
4 minutes before the quinoa is done cooking, stir in the broccoli
and scallions. Cover and set aside.

3. In a food processor, combine the drained cashews, white
beans, roasted red bell pepper, nutritional yeast, sherry, vinegar,
mustard, salt, and paprika. Process until smooth and well
blended. Add the almond milk and process until smooth.

4. Transfer the cooked quinoa mixture to the prepared baking
dish. Add the cashew mixture and mix well to combine. Spread
evenly in the baking dish and sprinkle with the bread crumbs.

5. Bake for about 30 minutes, or until the crumbs are golden
brown.

Manchurian Chickpeas

SERVES 4

Serve these zesty chickpeas over freshly cooked rice. Roasted cauliflower makes a great addition to the chickpeas—simply give bite-size cauliflower florets a 10-minute head start in the oven in the baking dish, then add the chickpeas and sauce and continue with the recipe.

- 1 tablespoon olive oil, or 2 tablespoons water
- 1 large yellow onion, finely chopped
- 3 garlic cloves, minced
- 2 teaspoons finely grated fresh ginger
- ½ teaspoon ground coriander
- ¼ teaspoon ground cumin
- ¼ teaspoon cayenne pepper
- 3 tablespoons tomato paste
- 3 tablespoons ketchup
- 3 tablespoons soy sauce
- 2 teaspoons dark (toasted) sesame oil
- 1 cup water
- 3 cups cooked or 2 (15.5-ounce) cans chickpeas, drained and rinsed
- 3 scallions, minced
- 2 tablespoons chopped fresh cilantro

1. Preheat the oven to 375°F. Lightly oil a 9- x 13-inch baking dish or line it with parchment paper.

2. Heat the oil in a large skillet over medium heat. Add the onion, cover, and cook until softened, stirring occasionally, about 5 minutes. Add the garlic, ginger, coriander, cumin, and cayenne, and cook for 1 to 2 minutes. Stir in the tomato paste, ketchup, soy sauce, and sesame oil. Stir in the water and cook, stirring, for 1 minute to blend the flavors. Remove from the heat. Add the chickpeas to the skillet, stirring gently to coat with the sauce. Spread the chickpea mixture evenly in the prepared baking dish. Bake until the sauce glazes onto the chickpeas, about 15 minutes. Serve hot, garnished with the scallions and cilantro.

Vegetable Fried Rice

SERVES 4

For best results, use cold cooked long-grain rice and your rice grains will remain fluffy and separate. Fried rice is a delicious reason to plan ahead and make extra rice whenever you're cooking some up. Cooked rice freezes well, so keep a container in the freezer.

1 tablespoon grapeseed oil
1 yellow onion, finely chopped
1 large carrot, shredded
3 scallions, minced
1 zucchini, finely chopped
2 garlic cloves, minced
2 teaspoons grated fresh ginger
3 cups cold cooked rice
1 cup frozen green peas, thawed
3 tablespoons soy sauce, plus more if needed
2 teaspoons mirin or white wine
1 tablespoon dark (toasted) sesame oil

Heat the oil in a large skillet over medium-high heat. Add the onion and carrot and stir-fry until softened, about 5 minutes. Add the scallions, zucchini, garlic, and ginger and stir-fry for 3 minutes. Add the rice, peas, soy sauce, and mirin and stir-fry until hot, about 5 minutes. Drizzle on the sesame oil, toss to combine, and taste and adjust the seasonings, adding more soy sauce if needed.

Polenta with Spicy Tomato-Mushroom Ragù

SERVES 4

For an even quicker version, use precooked polenta, available in the produce section of well-stocked supermarkets. Cut it into slices and sauté in a skillet in a small amount of olive oil, then top with the sauce.

1½ cups polenta or coarse-ground cornmeal
½ teaspoon salt
1 tablespoon olive oil
1 yellow onion, chopped
3 garlic cloves, chopped
8 ounces white or cremini mushrooms, chopped
3 cups marinara sauce
1 teaspoon ground fennel seeds
1 teaspoon dried basil
½ teaspoon red pepper flakes
½ teaspoon dried marjoram

1. Bring 6 cups water to a boil in a large pot. Slowly stream in the polenta and add the salt, whisking constantly. Decrease the heat to medium-low and continue whisking until the polenta pulls away from the sides of the pot, about 20 minutes. Keep warm.

2. Heat the oil in a saucepan over medium heat. Add the onion, cover, and cook until softened, 5 minutes. Add the garlic and mushrooms and cook until softened, about 3 minutes. Stir in the marinara sauce, fennel seeds, basil, red pepper flakes, and marjoram. Decrease the heat to low and simmer for 10 minutes. To serve, spoon the warm polenta into shallow bowls and top with the sauce.

Italian Truck-Stop Artichoke Risotto

SERVES 4

Inspired by a sublime risotto my husband enjoyed at a truck-stop restaurant in the middle of Tuscany, I have created this version so he can have it without traveling to Italy. Since fresh artichokes are prohibitively expensive for most of us to chop up in a recipe, the frozen variety works just fine. You can use canned artichoke hearts if you prefer; just be sure they are water packed and not the jarred marinated variety, as the flavor would be too strong.

2 tablespoons olive oil
1½ cups frozen artichoke hearts, thawed and chopped
2 garlic cloves, minced
1½ cups Arborio rice
½ cup dry white wine
4½ cups vegetable broth, heated
   Salt and freshly ground black pepper
¼ cup chopped fresh basil

Heat the oil in a large saucepan over medium heat. Add the artichoke hearts and garlic. Cover and cook for 5 minutes. Add the rice and stir to coat with the oil. Add the wine and stir gently until the liquid has been absorbed. Add the broth 1 cup at a time, stirring until the liquid has been absorbed before the next addition. Add salt and pepper to taste. Simmer until the desired consistency is reached, about 30 minutes. Add the basil; taste and adjust the seasonings, if needed. Serve immediately.

Kale and Red Beans with Olives and Lemon

SERVES 4

This recipe is a spin-off of a childhood favorite: escarole and white beans. In this version, I use kale instead of escarole and mahogany-colored kidney beans instead of white beans. For extra flavor, I've added Kalamata olives and lemon zest. It can be served over whole grains or pasta, or alone with toasted garlic bread.

     1   tablespoon olive oil
     1   large onion, chopped
         Salt and freshly ground black pepper
     3   garlic cloves, minced
     1   teaspoon dried basil
    ½   teaspoon dried oregano
    ¼   teaspoon red pepper flakes
     2   cups vegetable broth
    10   ounces kale, stemmed and chopped
   1½   cups cooked or 1 (15.5-ounce) can dark red kidney beans
           or other red beans, drained and rinsed
    ½   cup pitted Kalamata olives, halved
     2   teaspoons grated lemon zest

Heat the oil in a large pot or Dutch oven over medium heat. Add the onion and season with salt and black pepper. Cook until softened, 5 minutes. Stir in the garlic, basil, oregano, and red pepper flakes and cook for 30 seconds. Add the broth and bring to a boil. Stir in the kale, cover, and cook until wilted. Uncover and stir to mix well. Add the beans and more salt and pepper as needed, depending on the saltiness of your broth. Simmer until the kale is tender and the flavors have developed, about 10 minutes. Just before serving, drain off the liquid, then stir in the olives and lemon zest. Serve hot.

Moroccan-Spiced Chickpea and Sweet Potato Stew

SERVES 4 TO 6

Fragrant spices punctuate this mouthwatering stew that's thick with colorful vegetables, sweet potatoes, and chickpeas. Serve over couscous.

- 1 tablespoon olive oil
- 1 large yellow onion, chopped
- 1 large carrot, chopped
- 2 garlic cloves, minced
- 1 teaspoon grated fresh ginger
- 1 teaspoon ground coriander
- 1 teaspoon ground cumin
- ½ teaspoon ground turmeric
- ¼ teaspoon ground cinnamon
- ¼ teaspoon ground nutmeg
- 2 large sweet potatoes, peeled and diced
- 8 ounces green beans, trimmed and cut into 1-inch lengths
- 1½ cups cooked or 1 (15.5-ounce) can chickpeas, drained and rinsed
- 1 (14.5-ounce) can diced tomatoes, undrained
- 1½ cups water or vegetable broth
  Salt and freshly ground black pepper
- 2 tablespoons minced fresh parsley or cilantro
- 1 teaspoon fresh lemon juice

1. Heat the oil in a large pot over medium heat. Add the onion, carrot, garlic, and ginger. Cover and cook until softened, about 10 minutes. Stir in the coriander, cumin, turmeric, cinnamon, and nutmeg. Add the sweet potatoes, green beans, chickpeas, and tomatoes. Stir in the water and bring to a boil. Decrease the heat to low and season with salt and pepper to taste. Cover and simmer until the vegetables are tender, about 20 minutes.

2. Uncover, stir in the parsley and lemon juice, and cook for 10 minutes longer. Taste and adjust the seasonings, if needed. Serve hot.

Piccata-Style Cashew-Chickpea Medallions

SERVES 4

This easy and elegant dish is ideal for a special meal. The medallions can be made ahead and refrigerated until ready to cook. I like to serve them on top of freshly cooked rice with roasted asparagus.

    1 large garlic clove, crushed
    ¾ cup roasted cashews
    1 cup cooked or canned chickpeas, drained, rinsed, and blotted dry
    ¾ cup vital wheat gluten
    2 tablespoons soy sauce
    1 tablespoon water
    ½ teaspoon paprika
    ¼ teaspoon ground turmeric
    ¼ teaspoon salt
    2 tablespoons olive oil
    ¼ cup dry white wine
    2 tablespoons fresh lemon juice
    2 tablespoons minced fresh parsley
    1 tablespoon capers
       Salt and freshly ground black pepper

1. Combine the garlic and cashews in a food processor and process until finely ground. Add the chickpeas and pulse until broken up. Add the vital wheat gluten, soy sauce, water, paprika, turmeric, and salt and pulse until well mixed. Turn the mixture out of the processor and mix with your hands for a minute or two to fully incorporate. Divide the mixture into 8 pieces and shape into ½-inch-thick cutlets.

2. Heat the oil in a large skillet over medium heat. Add the cutlets and cook until browned, about 5 minutes per side. Add the wine, lemon juice, parsley, and capers. Season with salt and pepper to taste. Cook, turning once, until the liquid has reduced by half. Serve hot.

Pinto Bean and Sweet Potato Burritos

SERVES 6

The gorgeous colors of these baked burritos are surpassed only by their great flavor. If you don't have any baked sweet potatoes already on hand, you can cook some quickly in a microwave oven.

- 1 tablespoon olive oil
- 4 garlic cloves, minced
- ¼ teaspoon red pepper flakes (optional)
- 4 cups chopped Swiss chard, kale, spinach, or other dark greens
- 3 cups cooked or 2 (15.5-ounce) cans pinto beans, drained and rinsed
- ½ teaspoon salt
- 2 baked sweet potatoes, peeled and coarsely chopped
- 1 (16-ounce) jar salsa verde or tomato salsa
- 6 whole wheat tortillas

1. Preheat the oven to 350°F. Heat the oil in a large pot over medium heat. Add the garlic and red pepper flakes, if using, and cook until fragrant, about 30 seconds. Add the greens and cook for 5 minutes longer to wilt them. Stir in the beans and salt and then gently mix in the sweet potatoes.

2. Spread ¼ cup of the salsa verde in the bottom of a 9- x 11-inch baking dish. Place about 1 cup of the bean mixture in the center of a tortilla and roll up. Repeat with the remaining tortillas and bean mixture. Place the filled burritos in the baking dish, pour the remaining salsa verde over the top, and cover with aluminum foil. Bake until heated through, about 30 minutes.

Yellow Dal with Spinach

SERVES 4

Dal is a Hindi word for both the many varieties of beans, peas, and lentils and the dish that's made from them. The addition of baby spinach and chopped tomato adds lively streaks of green and red to the savory yellow puree.

1½ cups dried yellow split peas, picked through and rinsed
3 cups water
1 teaspoon salt
3 cups baby spinach
2 plum tomatoes, finely chopped
¼ cup chopped fresh cilantro
1 tablespoon canola or grapeseed oil
2 garlic cloves, minced
1 tablespoon finely chopped fresh ginger
1 small hot green chile, seeded and minced
1 teaspoon ground cumin
½ teaspoon ground coriander
½ teaspoon ground turmeric
2 teaspoons fresh lemon juice

1. Soak the split peas in water to cover for 1 hour. Drain, then transfer to a saucepan with the 3 cups water. Bring to a boil. Add the salt, decrease the heat to medium, and cook until tender and thickened, 30 to 40 minutes. (If your split peas are on the large side, they may take a bit longer to cook. If so, you will need to add an extra ½ cup water to finish cooking.) Stir in the spinach, tomatoes, and cilantro, stirring to wilt the spinach. Keep warm over very low heat.

2. Heat the oil in a small skillet over medium heat. Add the garlic, ginger, and chile. Heat until fragrant, about 1 minute. Remove from the heat and stir in the cumin, coriander, turmeric, and lemon juice, stirring to mix well. Add the spice mixture to the dal, stirring to combine. Serve hot.

Black Beans with Serrano Aioli

SERVES 4

The spicy aioli adds a creamy heat to the black beans. For a variation, add cooked rice to the bean mixture. If you prefer a less spicy version, cut back on the amount of serrano chile in the aioli.

- 1 serrano chile, seeded and diced
- 1 garlic clove, crushed
- ½ cup vegan mayonnaise
- 3 tablespoons fresh lemon juice
- ¼ teaspoon sugar
- ¼ cup olive oil
  Salt and freshly ground black pepper
- 3 cups cooked or 2 (15.5-ounce) cans black beans, drained and rinsed
- 2 tomatoes, chopped
- ¼ cup chopped fresh cilantro

1. In a food processor, combine the chile and garlic and process until finely minced. Add the mayonnaise, lemon juice, and sugar. With the machine running, add the oil in a stream, processing until the mixture is like a thin mayonnaise. Season with salt and pepper to taste. Refrigerate until ready to use.

2. Combine the black beans and tomatoes in a small saucepan and heat until hot. Season with salt and pepper to taste. To serve, spread the bean and tomato mixture into a shallow bowl. Drizzle with the aioli and garnish with the cilantro.

Three-Bean Cassoulet

SERVES 4 TO 6

Since cassoulet is all about white beans, I use three different kinds in this recipe. The size difference and subtle taste variance add interest. If you like vegan sausage links, cut some into ½-inch slices and sauté in a little oil to add to the cassoulet.

- 1 tablespoon olive oil
- 2 large carrots, chopped
- 1 large yellow onion, chopped
- 1 celery rib, chopped
- 3 garlic cloves, minced
- 1½ cups cooked or 1 (15.5-ounce) cans navy beans, drained and rinsed
- 1½ cups cooked or 1 (15.5-ounce) cans great northern beans, drained and rinsed
- 1½ cups cooked or 1 (15.5-ounce) cans cannellini beans, drained and rinsed
- 1 (14.5-ounce) can crushed tomatoes
- 1 cup water or vegetable broth
- 1 tablespoon minced fresh parsley
- 1 teaspoon dried savory
- 1 teaspoon dried thyme
- 1 teaspoon salt
- ¼ teaspoon freshly ground black pepper
- ½ cup dried bread crumbs

1. Preheat the oven to 375°F. Lightly oil a 2½-quart casserole dish. Heat the oil in a large skillet over medium heat. Add the carrots, onion, celery, and garlic. Cover and cook until softened, about 10 minutes. Transfer the vegetable mixture to the casserole dish. Stir in all of the beans, the tomatoes, water, parsley, savory, thyme, salt, and pepper. Cover tightly and bake for 45 minutes, or until the vegetables are tender and the flavors are blended.

2. Remove the cassoulet from the oven, uncover, and top with the bread crumbs. Return to the oven, uncovered, and bake for 10 minutes longer to lightly brown the crumbs.

Beans Bourguignon

SERVES 4

The common kidney bean gets star treatment in this oh-so-French stew made with lots of red wine and thickened with a vegan beurre manié. It is, of course, best served with crusty French bread and dry red wine.

- 2 tablespoons vegan butter
- 2 tablespoons all-purpose flour
- 1 tablespoon olive oil
- 3 shallots, diced
- 8 ounces carrots, cut diagonally into ¼-inch slices
- 2 garlic cloves, minced
- 1 cup vegetable broth or water
- 12 ounces white mushrooms, quartered
- 1½ cups dry red wine
- 1 cup canned crushed tomatoes
- 1 teaspoon dried thyme
- 1 bay leaf
- 3 cups cooked or 2 (15.5-ounce) cans dark red kidney beans, drained and rinsed
- Salt and freshly ground black pepper

1. Combine the butter and flour in a small bowl and knead until incorporated to make beurre manié. Refrigerate until needed.

2. Heat the oil in a large saucepan over medium heat. Add the shallots, carrots, and garlic. Cook, stirring, for 1 minute. Add ¼ cup of the broth and cook for 3 minutes longer to soften. Add the mushrooms and cook for 5 minutes longer. Stir in ½ cup of the wine, the remaining ¾ cup broth, the tomatoes, thyme, and bay leaf. Bring to a boil, then decrease the heat to low, cover, and simmer until the vegetables are cooked, about 30 minutes.

3. Add the remaining 1 cup wine, the beans, and salt and pepper to taste. Return to a boil, then decrease the heat to low and simmer, uncovered, for about 10 minutes. While the stew is simmering, pinch off pieces of the reserved beurre manié and add it to the stew, stirring after each addition to thicken. Remove and discard the bay leaf before serving.

Red Bean Jambalaya

SERVES 4

Since red beans are also a popular Creole ingredient, I think they are the natural alternative to meat in this vegan jambalaya, the quintessential Creole dish that combines rice with a spicy tomato-based stew. For a hearty addition, sauté some diced seitan or sliced vegan sausage links, and add to the jambalaya during the last few minutes of cooking.

- 2 tablespoons olive oil
- 2 celery ribs, chopped
- 1 yellow onion, chopped
- 1 green bell pepper, seeded and chopped
- 3 garlic cloves, minced
- 3 cups cooked or 2 (15.5-ounce) cans dark red kidney beans, drained and rinsed
- 1 cup long-grain rice
- 1 (14.5-ounce) can diced tomatoes, drained
- 1 (14.5-ounce) can crushed tomatoes
- 1 (4-ounce) can mild green chiles, drained
- 1 teaspoon salt
- 1 teaspoon dried thyme
- ½ teaspoon dried marjoram
   Freshly ground black pepper
- 2½ cups water or vegetable broth
- 1 tablespoon chopped fresh parsley
   Tabasco sauce, for serving (optional)

1. Heat the oil in a large pot over medium heat. Add the celery, onion, bell pepper, and garlic. Cover and cook until softened, about 7 minutes. Stir in the beans, rice, diced tomatoes, crushed tomatoes, chiles, salt, thyme, marjoram, and pepper to taste. Add the water, cover, and simmer until the vegetables are soft and the rice is tender, 50 to 55 minutes.

2. Serve sprinkled with the parsley and a splash of Tabasco, if using.

Millet-Topped Lentil Shepherd's Pie

SERVES 4

Millet is a super-nutritious and flavorful grain that isn't nearly as popular as it should be. I hope this recipe can help change that. I especially like the way the millet smoothes over the top of the casserole to mimic the classic mashed potato topping of a shepherd's pie.

2½ cups water
     Salt
1   cup millet
1   tablespoon nutritional yeast
2   teaspoons vegan butter (optional)
1   tablespoon olive oil
2   carrots, chopped
1   yellow onion, chopped
2   garlic cloves, minced
1   (14.5-ounce) can diced tomatoes, drained and finely chopped
1   cup vegetable broth
1   cup chopped mushrooms (any kind)
½   cup lentils, picked over and rinsed
1   teaspoon dried thyme
1   teaspoon dried marjoram
     Freshly ground black pepper
1   cup fresh or frozen corn kernels
½   cup frozen peas
½   teaspoon paprika

1. Preheat the oven to 350°F. Lightly oil a 2½ quart casserole dish. Bring the water to a boil in a saucepan. Salt the water, add the millet, cover, and decrease the heat to low. Simmer until the millet is cooked, about 25 minutes. Stir in the nutritional yeast and butter, if using, and set aside.

2. Heat the oil in a large saucepan over medium heat. Add the carrots, onion, and garlic. Cover and cook until softened, about 10 minutes. Add the tomatoes, broth, mushrooms, lentils, thyme, marjoram, and salt and pepper to taste. Cover and simmer until the lentils are soft and the mixture has thickened, about 30 minutes, adding a little water if the mixture becomes too thick.

3. Stir in the corn and peas, then transfer the lentil mixture to the casserole dish. Top with the millet and sprinkle with the paprika. Bake until hot, 30 to 40 minutes.

The Pasta (and Noodle) Bowl

Pasta and noodle dishes are among the easiest, most economical, and delicious meals you can make. From the easy weeknight Stovetop Broccoli Mac and Cheesy (page 121) to the elegantly flavorful Creamy Artichoke and Spinach Gemelli (page 115), these comforting and satisfying dishes have broad appeal, making them a good choice when you have finicky family members or when company's coming. A tasty selection of Asian noodle dishes, such as Rice Noodles and Asparagus with Peanut Sauce (page 128) and Bok Choy and Ginger-Sesame Udon Noodles (page 123), round out this chapter.

Roasted Vegetable Lasagna

Linguine Puttanesca

Creamy Artichoke and Spinach Gemelli

Tricolor Rotini with White Walnut Pesto

Sicilian Penne with Tomatoes and Eggplant

Orecchiette with Broccoli Rabe

Lemon-Kissed Linguine with Garlicky White Bean Sauce

Stovetop Broccoli Mac and Cheesy

Creamy Cashew Fettuccine with Mushrooms and Peas

Bok Choy and Ginger-Sesame Udon Noodles

Pad Thai at Home

Chinese Noodles and Broccoli with Spicy Black Bean Sauce

Rice Noodles and Asparagus with Peanut Sauce

Roasted Vegetable Lasagna

SERVES 6 TO 8

Thin layers of roasted vegetables lend their rich flavors to the lasagna, melding with the tofu filling and noodles. Use regular (not silken) tofu for this recipe.

- 1 zucchini, cut into ⅛-inch slices
- 1 eggplant, cut into ⅛-inch slices
- 1 red bell pepper, seeded and chopped
- 2 tablespoons olive oil
  Salt and freshly ground black pepper
- 8 ounces lasagna noodles
- 1 pound firm tofu, drained, pressed, and patted dry
- 1 pound soft (not silken) tofu, drained, pressed, and patted dry
- ¼ cup nutritional yeast
- 2 tablespoons minced fresh parsley
- 3 cups tomato sauce, store-bought or homemade
- ¼ cup vegan Parmesan

1. Preheat the oven to 425°F. Lightly oil a baking sheet. Arrange the zucchini, eggplant, and bell pepper on the baking sheet. Drizzle with the olive oil and season with salt and black pepper to taste. Roast the vegetables until soft and lightly browned, about 20 minutes. Remove from the oven and set aside to cool. Lower the oven temperature to 350°F.

2. While the vegetables are roasting, cook the lasagna noodles according to the package directions. Drain and set aside.

3. Crumble the firm and soft tofu into a large bowl. Add the nutritional yeast, parsley, and salt and black pepper to taste and mix well.

4. To assemble, spread a layer of the tomato sauce in the bottom of a 9- x 13-inch baking dish. Top the sauce with a layer of noodles. Top the noodles with half of the vegetables, then spread half the tofu mixture over the vegetables. Repeat with another layer of noodles, and top with more sauce. Repeat the layering process with the remaining vegetables and tofu mixture, ending with a layer of noodles and sauce. Sprinkle the vegan Parmesan on top. Cover and bake for 30 minutes. Remove the cover and bake for another 10 minutes. Let stand for 10 minutes before cutting.

Linguine Puttanesca

SERVES 4

This ultra-flavorful pasta dish made with lots of garlic, lusty olives, and piquant capers, all simmered in a rich tomato sauce, couldn't be easier to prepare. For a milder sauce, omit or cut back on the red pepper flakes.

- 2 tablespoons olive oil
- 5 garlic cloves, minced
- ½ teaspoon red pepper flakes
- ½ teaspoon dried oregano
- ½ teaspoon dried basil
- 1 (14.5-ounce) can crushed tomatoes
- 1 (14.5-ounce) can diced tomatoes, drained
  Salt and freshly ground black pepper
- ½ cup imported pitted black olives, halved
- ½ cup imported pitted green olives, halved
- 3 tablespoons capers
- 2 tablespoons minced fresh parsley
- 12 ounces linguine

1. Heat the oil in a saucepan over medium heat. Add the garlic and cook until fragrant, about 30 seconds. Stir in the red pepper flakes, oregano, and basil. Add the crushed tomatoes and diced tomatoes, and season with salt and black pepper to taste. Bring the sauce to a boil, then decrease the heat to low and simmer for 15 minutes, stirring occasionally. Stir in the black olives, green olives, capers, and parsley. Keep warm.

2. Bring a large pot of salted water to a boil and cook the linguine, stirring occasionally, until al dente. Drain the pasta and place in a shallow serving bowl. Add the sauce, toss to combine, and serve immediately.

Creamy Artichoke and Spinach Gemelli

SERVES 4

This is my go-to pasta dish when company's coming. The opulently creamy sauce and chewy pasta combine with fresh spinach, robust sun-dried tomatoes, and briny olives and artichokes for a captivating flavor combination.

  3 garlic cloves, crushed
  2 cups vegetable broth or almond milk
  2 tablespoons dry white wine
  ½ teaspoon dried oregano
  ½ teaspoon dried basil
 12 ounces gemelli or other bite-size pasta
  4 cups baby spinach, coarsely chopped
  1 tablespoon olive oil
  2 (8-ounce) jars marinated artichoke hearts, drained and chopped
  3 scallions, minced
  ¼ cup pitted Kalamata olives, coarsely chopped
  ¼ cup reconstituted or oil-packed sun-dried tomatoes, chopped
  1 (8-ounce) container vegan cream cheese, at room temperature
  ⅓ cup nutritional yeast
  2 tablespoons fresh lemon juice
     Salt and freshly ground black pepper
  2 tablespoons chopped fresh basil or parsley

1. In a saucepan, combine the garlic, broth, wine, oregano, and dried basil. Simmer for 5 minutes to blend the flavors. Keep warm.

2. Bring a large pot of salted water to a boil and cook the pasta, stirring occasionally, until al dente. Stir in the spinach, then drain well and return to the pot. Add the olive oil, artichoke hearts, scallions, olives, and tomatoes. Toss gently to combine. Keep warm.

3. In a food processor, combine the cream cheese, nutritional yeast, lemon juice, broth mixture, and salt and pepper to taste. Process until smooth and well blended.

4. Transfer the sauce to the pot containing the cooked pasta and vegetables. Add the fresh basil and mix gently to combine. Heat gently, and serve hot.

Tricolor Rotini with White Walnut Pesto

SERVES 4

Creamy and flavorful, this pesto bianco lightly cloaks the colorful rotini. The addition of green peas and sprinkling of parsley provides a lovely color contrast.

- 3 garlic cloves
- 3/4 cup walnut pieces
- 1 teaspoon salt
- 1 cup cooked white beans
- 1 cup plain unsweetened almond or soy milk
- 1/4 cup olive oil
- 12 ounces tricolor rotini
- 1 cup frozen green peas, thawed
- 2 tablespoons chopped fresh parsley or basil

1. Place the garlic, walnuts, and salt in a food processor and process to a paste. Add the beans and almond milk and process until well blended. With the machine running, slowly stream in the olive oil.

2. Bring a large pot of salted water to a boil and cook the rotini, stirring occasionally, until al dente. Stir in the peas, then drain and return to the pot. Add the pesto and toss gently to combine. Taste and adjust the seasonings, if needed. Sprinkle with the parsley and serve immediately.

Sicilian Penne with Tomatoes and Eggplant

SERVES 4

In Sicily, pasta dishes made with eggplant are called *alla Norma*. While it is said that this name honors the Bellini opera of the same name, some food writers note that the word *norma* in the Sicilian dialect means "normal." Thus, it can be inferred that pasta with eggplant is simply pasta in the "normal" way, since eggplant figures prominently in Sicilian cuisine.

- 2 tablespoons olive oil
- 1 yellow onion, chopped
- 3 garlic cloves, minced
- 1 eggplant, peeled and chopped
- 2 tablespoons tomato paste
- 1 (28-ounce) can diced tomatoes, drained
- 1/2 cup dry red wine
- 1 teaspoon dried marjoram
- 1/4 teaspoon red pepper flakes (optional)
  Salt and freshly ground black pepper
- 1 pound penne
- 2 tablespoons minced fresh basil

1. Heat the oil in a large saucepan over medium heat. Add the onion and garlic, cover, and cook until softened, about 5 minutes. Add the eggplant, cover, and cook for 5 minutes longer. Stir in the tomato paste, then add the tomatoes, wine, marjoram, and red pepper flakes, if using. Season with salt and black pepper to taste, then decrease the heat to low and simmer until the vegetables are soft and the sauce thickens, about 20 minutes. Taste and adjust the seasonings, if needed. Keep warm over low heat.

2. Bring a large pot of salted water to a boil and cook the penne, stirring occasionally, until al dente. Drain well and transfer to a shallow serving bowl. Add the sauce and toss to combine. Sprinkle with the basil and serve immediately.

Orecchiette with Broccoli Rabe

SERVES 4

Slightly chewy orecchiette, shaped like "little ears," comes from the Puglia region of southeastern Italy, where it is traditionally served with broccoli rabe or other green vegetable, such as arugula. A different pasta shape can be used instead of the orecchiette, if desired.

- 1 pound broccoli rabe (rapini), thick stems removed and discarded
- 4 tablespoons olive oil
- 4 garlic cloves, minced
- ¼ teaspoon red pepper flakes
  Salt and freshly ground black pepper
  Splash of white wine (optional)
- 1 pound orecchiette or other bite-size pasta

1. Coarsely chop the broccoli rabe. Heat 2 tablespoons of the oil in a medium pot over medium heat. Add the garlic and cook until fragrant, about 30 seconds. Add the broccoli rabe, red pepper flakes, and salt and black pepper to taste. Cook, stirring frequently, until the broccoli rabe is tender, about 5 minutes. Stir in about 1 tablespoon white wine, if using, and keep warm.

2. Bring a large pot of salted water to a boil and cook the pasta, stirring occasionally, until al dente. Drain the pasta and return it to the pot. Add the remaining 2 tablespoons olive oil and the broccoli rabe mixture and season with salt and black pepper to taste. Toss to combine and serve immediately.

Lemon-Kissed Linguine with Garlicky White Bean Sauce

SERVES 4

Creamy white cannellini beans, also known as white kidney beans, make this a satisfying and nutritious dish with a light sparkle of lemon.

- 3 tablespoons olive oil
- 4 large garlic cloves, minced
- 1½ cups cooked or 1 (15.5-ounce) can cannellini beans, drained and rinsed
- 2 tablespoons fresh lemon juice
- 1 tablespoon nutritional yeast (optional)
- ½ teaspoon dried oregano
- ½ teaspoon dried basil
- Salt and freshly ground black pepper
- 1 pound linguine
- 3 tablespoons minced fresh parsley

1. Heat the oil in large skillet over medium heat. Add the garlic and cook until fragrant, about 30 seconds. Add the beans, lemon juice, nutritional yeast (if using), oregano, basil, and salt and pepper to taste and cook until heated through, about 5 minutes. Keep warm.

2. Bring a large pot of salted water to a boil and cook the linguine, stirring occasionally, until al dente. Pour about ⅓ cup of the hot pasta water into the bean mixture. Drain the pasta and return it to the pot. Add the bean mixture and parsley and toss gently to combine. Serve immediately.

Stovetop Broccoli Mac and Cheesy

SERVES 4

This quick and easy "mac and cheese" is made on top of the stove, so there's no need to heat up the oven. However, if you don't plan to serve it right away, you can always put it in a casserole dish and keep it warm in a low oven.

12 ounces elbow macaroni or other bite-size pasta
4 cups small broccoli florets
¾ cup nutritional yeast
⅓ cup all-purpose flour
2 cups plain unsweetened soy or almond milk
1 tablespoon soy sauce
1 tablespoon fresh lemon juice
Salt and freshly ground black pepper

1. Bring a large pot of salted water to a boil and cook the pasta, stirring occasionally, until al dente. During the last 2 or 3 minutes of the cooking time, add the broccoli to the pasta and cook until it is almost tender.

2. In a saucepan over medium heat, combine the nutritional yeast and flour and cook, stirring, for 2 to 3 minutes. Slowly add the soy milk, stirring until smooth. Add the soy sauce, lemon juice, and salt and pepper to taste. Continue stirring until smooth and thickened.

3. When the pasta and broccoli are cooked, drain and return to the pot. Add the sauce and stir until well mixed. Serve hot.

Creamy Cashew Fettuccine with Mushrooms and Peas

SERVES 6

This decadently rich pasta dish gets its creamy goodness from the Creamy Cashew Sauce.

  2 tablespoons olive oil
  4 shallots, minced
 12 ounces white mushrooms, sliced
 ¼ cup dry sherry
  1 cup frozen baby peas, thawed
     Salt and freshly ground black pepper
 12 ounces fettuccine, broken into thirds
2½ cups Creamy Cashew Sauce (recipe follows)
  2 tablespoons minced fresh parsley

1. Heat the oil in a large skillet over medium heat. Add the shallots and cook until soft, about 5 minutes. Add the mushrooms and cook until softened, about 4 minutes. Add the sherry and cook, stirring, for 1 minute. Remove from the heat, stir in the peas, and season with salt and pepper to taste.

2. Bring a large pot of salted water to a boil and cook the fettuccine, stirring occasionally, until al dente. Drain the pasta and return it to the pot. Add the reserved mushroom and pea mixture along with the cashew sauce. Sprinkle with the parsley and serve hot.

Creamy Cashew Sauce

MAKES ABOUT 2½ CUPS

  1 cup raw cashews, soaked for 4 hours, then drained
  2 tablespoons nutritional yeast
 ½ teaspoon salt
  2 cups plain unsweetened almond milk

Grind the cashews in a high-speed blender. Add the nutritional yeast, salt, and 1 cup of the almond milk and blend until smooth. Add the remaining 1 cup almond milk and process until smooth.

Bok Choy and Ginger-Sesame Udon Noodles

SERVES 4

For a flavorful variation, add sliced shiitake mushrooms when you add the shallots and ginger.

1 head bok choy, cut crosswise into ¼-inch slices
12 ounces udon noodles
1 tablespoon dark (toasted) sesame oil
3 tablespoons tahini (sesame paste)
3 tablespoons soy sauce
3 tablespoons water
1½ tablespoons mirin
1 tablespoon grapeseed oil
½ cup thinly sliced shallots
1 tablespoon grated fresh ginger
¼ teaspoon red pepper flakes
1 tablespoon sesame seeds, toasted

1. Bring an inch or two of water to a simmer in a pot and lightly steam the bok choy over the simmering water until just tender, about 3 minutes. Set aside.

2. Bring a large pot of water to a boil and cook the udon according to the package directions. Drain and place in a bowl. Toss with the sesame oil and set aside.

3. In a small bowl, combine the tahini, soy sauce, water, and mirin, stirring to blend well.

4. Heat the grapeseed oil in a skillet or wok over medium-high heat. Add the shallots, ginger, and red pepper flakes and stir-fry for 1 minute. Add the bok choy, noodles, and sauce. Cook, stirring, until hot, 5 to 7 minutes. Serve immediately, sprinkled with the sesame seeds.

Pad Thai at Home

SERVES 4

Now you can make everyone's favorite Thai noodle dish in your own kitchen. Tamarind paste is available at Asian markets or online. If you can't find it, substitute 1 teaspoon molasses or brown sugar combined with 1 teaspoon lime juice. Be sure to use regular (not silken) tofu.

12	ounces dried rice noodles
1/3	cup soy sauce
3	tablespoons water
2	tablespoons fresh lime juice
2	tablespoons sugar
1	tablespoon tamarind paste
1	tablespoon tomato paste
1/2	teaspoon red pepper flakes
2	tablespoons grapeseed oil
1	pound extra-firm tofu, drained, pressed, and cut into 1/2-inch dice
1	small red onion, quartered and thinly sliced
4	scallions, minced
2	garlic cloves, minced
1/3	cup coarsely chopped dry-roasted peanuts
1/4	cup chopped fresh cilantro
1	cup fresh bean sprouts
1	lime, cut into wedges

1. Bring a large pot of water to a boil, add the rice noodles, and remove from the heat. Let the noodles soak until softened, 5 to 8 minutes depending on the thickness of the noodles. Drain and rinse under cold water. Transfer the drained noodles to a bowl and set aside.

2. In a bowl, combine the soy sauce, water, lime juice, sugar, tamarind paste, tomato paste, and red pepper flakes. Stir to mix well and set aside.

3. Heat 1 tablespoon of the grapeseed oil in a large nonstick skillet or wok over medium heat. Add the tofu and stir-fry until golden brown, about 5 minutes. Transfer to a platter.

CONTINUED ON PAGE 126

CONTINUED FROM PAGE 124

4. Reheat the same skillet or wok over medium heat with the remaining 1 tablespoon oil. Add the onion and stir-fry for 1 minute. Add the scallions and garlic, stir-fry for 30 seconds, then add the tofu and cook for about 7 minutes, tossing occasionally, until golden brown. Add the reserved noodles and toss to combine and heat through. Stir in the reserved sauce and cook, tossing to coat, adding a splash or two of additional water, if needed, to prevent sticking. When the noodles are hot and tender, mound them on a serving platter and sprinkle with the peanuts and cilantro. Garnish with the bean sprouts and lime wedges on the side on the platter. Serve hot.

Chinese Noodles and Broccoli with Spicy Black Bean Sauce

SERVES 4

This recipe is fast, easy, and delicious. You can vary this recipe by adding additional veggies: edamame and sliced carrots are good choices. If egg-free Chinese noodles are unavailable, use linguine or spaghetti.

- 8 ounces egg-free Chinese noodles or linguine
- 3 cups broccoli florets
- 1 teaspoon dark (toasted) sesame oil
- 1 tablespoon grapeseed oil
- 1 red onion, thinly sliced
- 1 garlic clove, minced
- 1 teaspoon grated fresh ginger
- ½ cup water
- 3 tablespoons black bean sauce
- 2 tablespoons soy sauce
- 1 teaspoon Asian chili paste
- 1 tablespoon cornstarch dissolved in 2 tablespoons water
- ¼ cup chopped roasted cashews

1. Bring a pot of water to a boil and cook the noodles according to the package directions. During the last few minutes of the cooking time, add the broccoli florets to lightly cook them. Drain, rinse, and place the noodles and broccoli in a large bowl. Toss with the sesame oil.

2. Heat the grapeseed oil in a wok or large skillet. Add the onion and stir-fry until soft, about 5 minutes. Add the garlic and ginger and stir-fry until fragrant, about 30 seconds. Stir in the water, black bean sauce, soy sauce, and chili paste. Simmer for 30 seconds to blend the flavors. Add the cornstarch mixture and stir to thicken. Add the noodles and broccoli and toss to coat with the sauce and heat through. Serve immediately, sprinkled with the cashews.

Rice Noodles and Asparagus with Peanut Sauce

SERVES 4

Chewy rice noodles pair well with fresh asparagus, both cloaked in a creamy peanut sauce, although any type of noodles may be used instead and steamed broccoli or green beans may replace the asparagus, if desired.

- 1 pound flat rice noodles or linguine
- 12 ounces asparagus, trimmed and cut into 1-inch pieces
- 1 tablespoon dark (toasted) sesame oil
- 1/2 cup creamy peanut butter
- 1/3 cup hot water
- 3 tablespoons soy sauce
- 1 tablespoon fresh lime juice
- 2 teaspoons sugar
- 1/2 teaspoon Asian chili paste
- 1 tablespoon grapeseed oil
- 1 small red onion, thinly sliced
- 1 small red bell pepper, seeded and thinly sliced
- 3 scallions, minced
- 2 garlic cloves, minced
- 1 teaspoon grated fresh ginger
- 2 tablespoons minced fresh cilantro
- 2 tablespoons chopped roasted peanuts

1. Bring a large pot of water to a boil and cook the noodles according to the package directions. During the last 5 minutes of the cooking time, add the asparagus to the pot. Drain well, return the noodles and asparagus to the pot, and toss with the sesame oil. Set aside.

2. In a bowl, combine the peanut butter, hot water, soy sauce, lime juice, sugar, and chili paste. Stir until the sugar is dissolved and the mixture is smooth, adding additional hot water, if needed, to make a smooth sauce.

3. Heat the grapeseed oil in a medium skillet over medium-high heat. Add the onion and bell pepper and cook, stirring, until softened, about 5 minutes. Add the scallions, garlic, and ginger, and cook, stirring, for 1 minute. Add the mixture to the pot with the pasta and asparagus. Add the peanut sauce and toss to coat. Transfer to individual plates or a large platter and sprinkle with the cilantro and peanuts.

Meaty Mains

This chapter spotlights the protein-rich stars of vegan cuisine with hearty recipes featuring tofu, tempeh, and seitan prepared in a variety of tantalizing ways, from Orange-Bourbon Tempeh (page 143) to Chipotle-Painted Baked Tofu (page 133) to Seitan with Prunes, Olives, and Capers (page 144). There's even a luscious meat loaf recipe and a creamy one-dish casserole bake.

One-Dish Dauphinoise

SERVES 4 TO 6

This delicious baked casserole includes everything you need for a satisfying one-dish meal. It features spinach, squash, potatoes, and your choice of plant-based protein, all combined in a creamy sauce and topped with vegan cheese.

- 2 teaspoons vegan butter
- 3 garlic cloves, minced
- 1/2 teaspoon dried thyme
- 1 cup vegan cream cheese
- 2 tablespoons cornstarch
- 1 cup plain unsweetened almond or soy milk
- 1 teaspoon Dijon mustard
  Salt and freshly ground black pepper
- 1/2 to 1 cup vegetable broth, as needed
- 1 tablespoon olive oil
- 1 small onion, minced
- 8 cups chopped spinach or kale
  Choice of protein: 1½ cups cooked white beans, cooked green lentils, chopped reconstituted Soy Curls, or chopped seitan
- 1½ pounds russet potatoes, peeled and cut into 1/8-inch-thick slices
- 1 pound butternut squash, peeled and cut into 1/4-inch-thick slices
- 1/2 cup shredded vegan mozzarella

1. Preheat the oven to 375°F. Thoroughly oil a 9- x 13-inch baking dish. Melt the butter in a small skillet over medium heat. Add the garlic and thyme and cook for about 3 minutes to soften.

2. Transfer the garlic mixture to a food processor or blender. Add the cream cheese, cornstarch, almond milk, mustard, and salt and pepper to taste. Add as much of the broth as needed to make a smooth sauce. Set aside.

3. Heat the oil in a skillet over medium heat. Add the onion and cook until softened, 5 minutes. Add the spinach and salt and pepper to taste. Cook, stirring, until wilted, then add the white beans (or other protein) and continue to cook until the mixture is well blended. Remove from the heat.

4. Spread a thin layer of the sauce in the bottom of the prepared baking dish. Spread a layer of potatoes and squash slices over the sauce. Spread the spinach and bean mixture evenly over the potato and squash layer, then add a light sprinkling of mozzarella and season with salt and pepper. Top with a layer of sauce, and continue layering until all of the potatoes, squash, and cheese sauce have been used, ending with a layer of sauce and a final sprinkle of cheese. Cover with aluminum foil and bake until the potatoes and squash are tender, 1 hour. Remove the foil and bake for 10 minutes longer. Let rest for 10 minutes before serving.

My Kinda Meat Loaf

SERVES 6

This wholesome loaf combines regular (not silken) tofu, oats, and vital wheat gluten with walnuts and tahini for a nutritious, protein-packed vegan "meat loaf" that is great topped with brown gravy and served with oven-roasted potatoes and vegetables for a nostalgic comfort-food meal. Instead of baking it in a loaf pan, it can also be shaped into a loaf and baked in an oiled baking dish.

1 tablespoon plus 1 teaspoon olive oil
½ cup minced onion
1 garlic clove, minced
1 pound extra-firm tofu, drained and crumbled
1 tablespoon soy sauce
½ cup ground walnuts
2 tablespoons tahini (sesame paste) or peanut butter
1 cup vital wheat gluten
¾ cup old-fashioned rolled oats
1 tablespoon minced fresh parsley
1 teaspoon salt
¾ teaspoon paprika
¼ teaspoon freshly ground black pepper

1. Preheat the oven to 375°F. Lightly oil a 9- x 5-inch loaf pan.

2. Heat the 1 tablespoon of the oil in a large skillet over medium heat. Add the onion and garlic, cover, and cook until softened, 5 minutes. Add the tofu and soy sauce and cook, stirring, for 5 minutes. Add the walnuts, tahini, vital wheat gluten, oats, parsley, salt, ½ teaspoon of the paprika, and pepper, and mix well. If the mixture seems too dry, add a little water, 2 tablespoons at a time, then transfer the mixture to the prepared pan. Press the mixture firmly into the pan, smoothing the top. Sprinkle the remaining ¼ teaspoon paprika on top and drizzle with the remaining 1 teaspoon oil, rubbing the top of the loaf to coat. Bake until firm and golden brown, 50 to 60 minutes, checking after around 40 minutes; if the top is getting too brown, cover with aluminum foil for the remaining baking time. Uncover and let stand for 10 minutes before slicing.

Chipotle-Painted Baked Tofu

SERVES 4

If you like the smoky heat of chipotle chiles, then you'll love what it does for tofu. A little chipotle goes a long way, but there's no need to waste the rest when opening a can for just a small amount. Simply measure out what you need and then freeze the rest in small measured amounts for use in future recipes. Be sure to use regular (not silken) tofu in this recipe.

1 **pound extra-firm tofu, drained and cut into ½-inch-thick slices**
¼ **cup soy sauce**
2 **canned chipotle chiles in adobo sauce**
1 **tablespoon agave nectar or pure maple syrup**
1 **tablespoon olive oil**

1. Preheat the oven to 375°F. Lightly oil a shallow baking pan or line it with parchment paper. Press the liquid out of the tofu slices. In a blender or food processor, combine the soy sauce, chiles, agave, and oil and process until blended.

2. Brush the chipotle mixture onto both sides of the tofu slices and arrange them in a single layer in the prepared baking pan. Bake until hot and glazed with the sauce, about 20 minutes.

Country-Fried Tofu with Golden Gravy

SERVES 4

The rich, golden gravy is made with pureed chickpeas for a wholesome and satisfying sauce to cloak the crisply fried tofu. Use regular (not silken) tofu.

- 1 pound extra-firm tofu, drained and cut into ½-inch slices
  Salt and freshly ground black pepper
- ½ cup cornstarch
- 1 teaspoon smoked paprika
- 3 tablespoons olive oil
- 1 sweet yellow onion, chopped
- 2 tablespoons all-purpose flour
- ½ teaspoon dried thyme
- ¼ teaspoon ground turmeric
- ¼ teaspoon cayenne pepper
- 1½ cups plain unsweetened almond or soy milk, plus more if needed
- 1 cup cooked or canned chickpeas, drained and rinsed
- 2 tablespoons minced fresh parsley

1. Preheat the oven to 250°F. Cover a large baking sheet with paper towels. Place the tofu slices in a single layer on the towels. Cover the tofu with paper towels and press down on the tofu to remove the excess liquid. Remove and discard the paper towels. Season the tofu with salt and pepper to taste. Place the cornstarch and paprika in a shallow bowl. Dredge the tofu in the cornstarch mixture, coating all sides.

2. Heat 2 tablespoons of the oil in a large nonstick skillet over medium heat. Add the tofu, in batches as necessary, and cook until golden brown on both sides. Transfer the tofu to an ovenproof platter and keep warm in the oven.

3. In the same skillet, heat the remaining 1 tablespoon oil over medium heat. Add the onion, cover, and cook for 5 minutes, or until softened. Uncover and decrease the heat to low. Stir in the flour, thyme, turmeric, and cayenne and cook for 1 minute, stirring constantly. Slowly add the almond milk, whisking constantly. Add the chickpeas and season with salt and pepper to taste. Continue to cook for 2 minutes, stirring frequently. Transfer to a blender and process until smooth and creamy. Return to the skillet and heat until hot, adding a little more almond milk if the sauce is too thick. To serve, spoon the sauce over the tofu and sprinkle with the parsley.

"Ka-Pow" Tofu

SERVES 4

When I order tofu kaprao in my favorite Thai restaurant, I know it will contain the wonderfully fragrant Thai basil. I also know it will pack a spicy punch, so I've come to call it "ka-pow." If the sublime Thai basil is unavailable, there's no exact substitute, although you could use regular basil or cilantro and still have a tasty meal. Vegan oyster sauce (sold as vegetarian oyster sauce or mushroom soy sauce) is available at Asian markets or online. If you can't find it, leave it out and add a little extra soy sauce. Use regular (not silken) tofu. This is delicious served over jasmine rice.

1 pound extra-firm tofu, drained and patted dry
Salt and freshly ground black pepper
2 tablespoons cornstarch
3 tablespoons soy sauce
1 tablespoon vegan oyster sauce
1 teaspoon rice vinegar
1 teaspoon sugar
½ teaspoon red pepper flakes
2 tablespoons grapeseed oil
1 sweet yellow onion, halved lengthwise and thinly sliced
1 red bell pepper, seeded and thinly sliced
3 scallions, chopped
½ cup fresh Thai basil leaves

1. Cut the tofu into 1-inch cubes and place in a bowl. Season with salt and black pepper to taste, sprinkle with the cornstarch, and toss to coat. In a small bowl, combine the soy sauce, oyster sauce, vinegar, sugar, and red pepper flakes. Stir well to combine and set aside.

2. Heat 1 tablespoon of the oil in a large skillet over medium-high heat. Add the tofu and cook until golden brown. Remove from the skillet.

3. Heat the remaining 1 tablespoon oil in the same skillet. Add the onion and bell pepper and stir-fry until softened, about 5 minutes. Add the scallions and cook for 1 minute longer. Stir in the tofu, the sauce, and the basil and stir-fry until hot, about 3 minutes.

Thai-phoon Stir-Fry

SERVES 4

This spicy-sweet stir-fry of noodles, tofu, and vegetables is seasoned with all the fragrant and flavorful ingredients of Thai cuisine. I call it "Thai-phoon" because the tasty garnishes are scattered on top as if by a strong wind. Use regular (not silken) tofu.

- 4 tablespoons soy sauce
- 1 tablespoon plus 1 teaspoon dark (toasted) sesame oil
- 2 teaspoons minced garlic
- 2 teaspoons grated fresh ginger
- 1 pound extra-firm tofu, drained and patted dry
- 1 tablespoon creamy peanut butter
- 2 teaspoons sugar
- 1/8 teaspoon cayenne pepper
- 1 (13.5-ounce) can unsweetened low-fat coconut milk
- 1 tablespoon fresh lime juice
- 1 tablespoon grapeseed oil
- 1 large shallot, slivered
- 8 ounces shiitake mushrooms, sliced
- 1 tablespoon mirin
- 6 ounces baby spinach
- 12 ounces rice noodles, soba noodles, or linguine
- 1/4 cup shredded unsweetened coconut, toasted
- 2 tablespoons finely chopped fresh basil
- 2 tablespoons crushed roasted peanuts
- 2 teaspoons minced crystallized ginger (optional)

1. In a shallow bowl, combine 3 tablespoons of the soy sauce with 1 tablespoon of the sesame oil, 1 teaspoon of the garlic, and 1 teaspoon of the ginger. Stir to combine. Cut the tofu into 1/2-inch dice and add to the marinade, tossing to combine. Let marinate for 1 hour, stirring occasionally.

2. In a saucepan, combine the peanut butter, sugar, cayenne, and the remaining 1 tablespoon soy sauce. Over medium heat, stir in the coconut milk until well blended. Add the marinated tofu cubes and any leftover marinade and bring to a simmer. Do not boil. Decrease the heat to medium-low, cover, and simmer for 15 minutes, stirring occasionally. Stir in the lime juice and keep warm.

3. Heat the grapeseed oil in a large skillet over medium heat. Add the shallot, remaining 1 teaspoon garlic, and remaining 1 teaspoon ginger and cook, stirring, for 2 minutes. Add the mushrooms and cook until they release their juices, about 5 minutes. Stir in the mirin, then add the spinach and continue stirring until wilted. Set aside and keep warm.

4. Bring a pot of water to a boil and cook the noodles according to the package directions. Drain and toss with the remaining 1 teaspoon sesame oil.

5. To assemble, divide the noodles among four plates. Top each with some of the shiitake-spinach mixture, followed by the tofu and coconut sauce. Garnish each plate with a sprinkling of toasted coconut, basil, peanuts, and crystallized ginger, if using.

Soy-tan Dream Cutlets

SERVES 4

I love to sauté both extra-firm tofu and seitan, but sometimes the texture isn't ideal—the tofu may not be firm enough or the seitan may be too chewy. My dream had long been to create a vegan cutlet with a texture that was "just right." This is it: these cutlets combine vital wheat gluten (used to make seitan) with tofu. They can be used in virtually any sauté or stir-fry recipe instead of using seitan, tempeh, or extra-firm tofu.

6 ounces extra-firm tofu, drained and pressed
2½ tablespoons soy sauce
½ teaspoon ground turmeric
½ teaspoon paprika
¼ teaspoon freshly ground black pepper
¾ cup vital wheat gluten
2 tablespoons olive oil

1. In a food processor, combine the tofu, soy sauce, turmeric, paprika, pepper, and vital wheat gluten. Process until well mixed. Turn the mixture onto a clean work surface and knead for 2 minutes. Divide into 4 pieces and flatten each piece into a very thin cutlet, no more than ¼ inch thick.

2. Heat the oil in a large skillet over medium heat. Add the cutlets and cook until nicely browned on both sides, about 5 minutes per side.

Creole Tempeh

SERVES 4 TO 6

Firm slices of tempeh stand up well to the lively Creole seasoning. Serve over rice and celebrate Mardi Gras.

- 2 (8-ounce) packages tempeh, thinly sliced
- ¼ cup soy sauce
- 3 tablespoons Creole seasoning blend
- ½ cup all-purpose flour
- 3 tablespoons olive oil
- 1 sweet yellow onion, chopped
- 1 red or green bell pepper, seeded and chopped
- 1 celery rib, chopped
- 2 garlic cloves, chopped
- 1 (14.5-ounce) can diced tomatoes, drained
- 2 bay leaves
- 1 teaspoon dried thyme
- ½ teaspoon dried basil
- ½ cup dry red wine
  Salt and freshly ground black pepper

1. Place the tempeh in a saucepan with enough water to cover. Add the soy sauce and 1 tablespoon of the Creole seasoning. Cover and simmer for 45 minutes. Remove the tempeh from the liquid, reserving the liquid.

2. In a shallow bowl, combine the flour with the remaining 2 tablespoons Creole seasoning and mix well. Dredge the tempeh in the flour mixture, coating well.

3. Heat 2 tablespoons of the oil in a large skillet over medium heat. Add the tempeh and cook until browned on both sides, in batches if necessary. Remove the tempeh from the skillet. Heat the remaining 1 tablespoon oil in the same skillet over medium heat. Add the onion, bell pepper, celery, and garlic. Cover and cook until the vegetables are softened, about 10 minutes. Stir in the tomatoes, then add the tempeh back to the skillet along with the bay leaves, thyme, basil, wine, and 1 cup of the reserved simmering liquid. Season with salt and black pepper to taste. Bring to a simmer and cook for about 30 minutes. Remove the bay leaves before serving.

Orange-Bourbon Tempeh

SERVES 4 TO 6

I adapted this recipe from one shared with me by my friend and vegan chef Tal Ronnen. Even people who think they don't like tempeh may change their minds when they taste this dish.

- 2 cups water
- ½ cup soy sauce
- 8 thin slices fresh ginger
- 2 garlic cloves, thinly sliced
- Zest of ½ orange
- Salt
- 2 (8-ounce) packages tempeh, cut into ½-inch strips
- Freshly ground black pepper
- ½ cup all-purpose flour
- 2 tablespoons grapeseed oil
- 1 tablespoon agave nectar
- ½ teaspoon dried thyme
- ⅓ cup fresh orange juice
- ¼ cup bourbon
- 4 or 5 orange slices, halved
- 2 teaspoons cornstarch mixed with 2 tablespoons water (optional)

1. In a saucepan, combine the water, soy sauce, ginger, garlic, orange zest, and ¼ teaspoon salt. Place the tempeh in the marinade and bring to a boil. Decrease the heat to low and simmer for 45 minutes. Remove the tempeh from the marinade, reserving the marinade liquid. Sprinkle the tempeh with salt and pepper to taste, then dredge it in the flour.

2. Heat the oil in a large skillet over medium heat. Add the tempeh, in batches if necessary, and cook until browned on both sides, about 4 minutes per side. Gradually stir in the reserved marinade. Add the agave, thyme, orange juice, and bourbon. Top the tempeh with the orange slices. Cover and simmer for 30 minutes.

3. Use a slotted spoon or spatula to remove the tempeh from the pan and transfer it to a serving platter. Keep warm. If you want a thicker sauce, add the cornstarch mixture and cook, stirring, to thicken the sauce. Decrease the heat to low and simmer, stirring constantly, until the sauce is thickened. Taste the sauce and adjust the seasonings, if needed. Spoon the sauce over the tempeh and serve hot.

Seitan with Prunes, Olives, and Capers

SERVES 4

This sweet and savory dish with the flavors of Morocco was inspired by a popular chicken recipe that made the rounds in the early 1980s. This is a fun dish to serve to guests if their tastes lean to the exotic. It's great served over rice, millet, or couscous, accompanied with a salad or sautéed greens.

- 3 tablespoons olive oil
- 12 ounces seitan, cut into thin slices
  Cornmeal, for dredging
  Salt and freshly ground black pepper
- 2 garlic cloves, minced
- ½ cup dry white wine
- ½ cup vegetable broth
- 2 tablespoons red wine vinegar
- 2 tablespoons sugar
- 1 teaspoon chopped fresh oregano or ½ teaspoon dried
- ¼ teaspoon red pepper flakes
- ¾ cup pitted prunes
- ½ cup pitted green olives
- ⅓ cup dried apricots, halved
- ¼ cup capers
- 2 tablespoons chopped fresh parsley

1. Preheat the oven to 250°F. Heat 2 tablespoons of the oil in a large skillet over medium heat. Dredge the seitan slices in cornmeal and add to the skillet, working in batches as needed. Season with salt and black pepper to taste and cook until browned. Transfer the seitan to a heatproof platter and keep warm in the oven.

2. Heat the remaining 1 tablespoon oil in the same skillet. Add the garlic and cook until fragrant, about 30 seconds. Stir in the wine, broth, vinegar, sugar, oregano, and red pepper flakes. Bring to a boil, stirring to dissolve the sugar. Decrease the heat to low and simmer until the liquid reduces slightly. Stir in the prunes, olives, apricots, and capers and cook until heated through, about 4 minutes. To serve, spoon the sauce over the seitan and sprinkle with the parsley.

Pan-Seared Seitan with Artichoke Hearts, Tomatoes, and Kalamata Olives

SERVES 4

Pungently redolent of olives, capers, and artichoke hearts, this full-flavored dish is terrific over freshly cooked rice or pasta, accompanied with spinach or kale sautéed in garlic and olive oil.

- 2 tablespoons olive oil
- 12 ounces seitan, cut into ¼-inch-thick slices
- 2 garlic cloves, minced
- 1 (14.5-ounce) can diced tomatoes, drained
- 1½ cups cooked (canned or frozen) artichoke hearts, sliced
- ⅓ cup pitted oil-cured black olives, halved
- 3 tablespoons chopped fresh parsley
- 1 tablespoon capers
  Salt and freshly ground black pepper

1. Preheat the oven to 250°F. Heat 1 tablespoon of the oil in a large skillet over medium-high heat. Add the seitan and brown on both sides, about 5 minutes. Remove the seitan from the pan and keep warm, covered, in the oven.

2. Heat the remaining 1 tablespoon oil in the same skillet over medium heat. Add the garlic and cook until fragrant, about 30 seconds. Add the tomatoes, artichoke hearts, olives, parsley, and capers. Season with salt and black pepper to taste and cook until hot, about 5 minutes. To serve, arrange the seitan on plates and top with the vegetable mixture.

On the Side

In my recipes, vegetables usually participate in main dishes; however, there are occasions when a vegetable side dish is in order. For such occasions, I've included some of the most delicious vegetable recipes imaginable, from fragrant Curry-Roasted Cauliflower (page 148) to Thyme-Scented Sweet Potatoes with Black Olives and Garlic (page 159). Some of the recipes, such as the Mediterranean Artichoke Sauté (page 151), Roasted Lemon Asparagus with Pine Nuts (page 149), and Roasted Zucchini and Tomatoes (page 163), can be easily transformed into one-dish meals with the addition of cooked beans (or other vegan protein) and served over rice, quinoa, or pasta.

Curry-Roasted Cauliflower

Roasted Lemon Asparagus with Pine Nuts

Broccoli with Black Beans and Walnuts

Mediterranean Artichoke Sauté

Spicy Sautéed Broccoli Rabe

Sesame Spinach

Emerald Mashed Potatoes

Potato Pancakes with Green Scallions

Thyme-Scented Sweet Potatoes with
    Black Olives and Garlic

Broccoli- and Cheddar-Stuffed Portobellos

Roasted Zucchini and Tomatoes

Curry-Roasted Cauliflower

SERVES 4

If you think you don't like cauliflower, please try it this way at least once and see if you don't change your mind. The best flavor comes from cooking it long enough so that it is tender and sweet inside and crisp and browned outside. The hint of curry adds an extra flavor dimension, but it's quite good without any added embellishment as well.

1 head cauliflower, cut into small uniform florets
2 tablespoons olive oil
1 tablespoon curry powder
  Salt and freshly ground black pepper
1 tablespoon fresh lemon juice
2 tablespoons minced fresh parsley or cilantro

1. Preheat the oven to 425°F. Line a baking sheet with aluminum foil or parchment paper.

2. In a large bowl, combine the cauliflower with the oil, curry powder, and salt and pepper to taste. Mix well to coat the cauliflower.

3. Arrange the cauliflower in a single layer on the prepared baking sheet. Roast until the cauliflower is tender and slightly browned, turning a few times to brown evenly, about 30 minutes. Serve hot, sprinkled with the lemon juice and parsley.

Roasted Lemon Asparagus with Pine Nuts

SERVES 4

If you've never eaten roasted asparagus, you don't know what you're missing. Roasting produces the absolute best-tasting asparagus on earth, bringing out its natural flavor and, at the same time, adding a bit of crispness to the tips. The addition of lemon and pine nuts makes a great dish even better.

- 1 **pound thin asparagus**
- 2 **tablespoons olive oil**
  Salt and freshly ground black pepper
- 1 **garlic clove, minced**
- ¼ **cup pine nuts**
- 1 **tablespoon fresh lemon juice**

Preheat the oven to 425°F. Lightly oil a large baking pan or line it with parchment paper. Spread the asparagus in a single layer in the prepared pan. Drizzle with the olive oil and season with salt and pepper to taste. Sprinkle with the garlic and pine nuts and roast until the asparagus is tender, about 10 minutes. Transfer to a platter and sprinkle with the lemon juice.

Broccoli with Black Beans and Walnuts

SERVES 4 TO 6

One might think it's enough that this side dish is bright, colorful, and loaded with flavor. But it doesn't stop there—it's also loaded with vitamin C, calcium, iron, and lots of other important nutrients. As is, this is a hearty side dish for four to six people; if you serve this over rice, it can be enjoyed as a one-dish meal for two or three people.

- 2 tablespoons olive oil
- 4 to 5 cups small broccoli florets
- 2 garlic cloves, minced
- 2 scallions, chopped
- 1 to 1½ cups cooked or canned black beans, drained and rinsed
- ⅓ cup chopped walnuts
- 2 tablespoons chopped fresh parsley
  Salt and freshly ground black pepper

Heat the oil in a large skillet over medium heat. Add the broccoli and cook, stirring, until just tender, about 7 minutes. Stir in the garlic and scallions and cook for 1 minute longer. Stir in the black beans, walnuts, and parsley. Season with salt and pepper to taste. Cook until hot, about 3 minutes.

Mediterranean Artichoke Sauté

SERVES 4

Fresh artichokes are prohibitively expensive for most of us, but frozen artichoke hearts can be quite flavorful, especially when combined with a retinue of Mediterranean ingredients.

- 1 (9-ounce) bag frozen artichoke hearts, thawed
- 2 tablespoons olive oil
- 2 shallots, chopped
- 2 garlic cloves, minced
- 1 red bell pepper, seeded and cut into julienne strips
- 2 tablespoons white wine
- 2 tablespoons water
    Salt and freshly ground black pepper
- 2 plum tomatoes, diced
- ¼ cup imported pitted black olives, coarsely chopped
- 1 tablespoon capers
- 2 tablespoons torn fresh basil leaves

Quarter the artichoke hearts. Heat the oil in a large skillet over medium heat. Add the shallots, cover, and cook for 3 minutes. Stir in the garlic and cook for 1 minute. Add the red bell pepper, artichokes, white wine, and water and season with salt and black pepper to taste. Cover and simmer until the vegetables are tender, 10 minutes. Stir in the tomatoes, olives, and capers and cook until the vegetables are hot and the liquid is absorbed, about 5 minutes. Add the basil and toss to combine.

Spicy Sautéed Broccoli Rabe

SERVES 4

Popular in Italy, this bitter green vegetable, also known as rapini, is becoming more common in the United States. If broccoli rabe is unavailable, use spinach, Swiss chard, escarole, or any dark leafy green.

1 **bunch broccoli rabe (rapini), tough stems removed**
2 **tablespoons olive oil**
3 **garlic cloves, minced**
½ **teaspoon red pepper flakes**
   Salt and freshly ground black pepper

1. Bring a saucepan of salted water to a boil and cook the broccoli rabe until just tender, 3 to 5 minutes. Drain and run under cold water to stop the cooking, then coarsely chop.

2. Heat the oil in a large skillet over medium heat. Add the garlic and cook for 30 seconds. Stir in the broccoli rabe and red pepper flakes. Season with salt and black pepper to taste and cook, stirring, until heated through, about 3 minutes.

Sesame Spinach

SERVES 4

This recipe is inspired by the Japanese salad called *gomae* made with chilled spinach and a tahini dressing. Instead of a salad, it's presented here as a hot side dish.

- ¼ cup tahini (sesame paste)
- 2 tablespoons fresh lemon juice
- 1 tablespoon dark (toasted) sesame oil
- 1 garlic clove, minced
- Salt and freshly ground black pepper
- 8 cups baby spinach
- 1 tablespoon black sesame seeds

1. In a blender or food processor, combine the tahini, lemon juice, sesame oil, garlic, and salt and pepper to taste. Blend until smooth. If the sauce is too thick, add up to 2 tablespoons water.

2. Place the spinach in a large pot with 2 tablespoons water over medium heat. Cover and cook until wilted, stirring occasionally, 3 to 4 minutes. Season with salt and pepper to taste. Transfer the spinach to a bowl and drizzle with the tahini sauce. Sprinkle with the sesame seeds.

Emerald Mashed Potatoes

SERVES 6

Reminiscent of the Irish potato and kale dish known as colcannon, this version has a decidedly non-Irish twist with the added splash of umeboshi vinegar and flaxseed oil. If umeboshi vinegar is unavailable, use brown rice vinegar instead.

- 6 large Yukon Gold potatoes, peeled and cut into chunks
- 4 cups finely shredded kale
- 1 tablespoon flaxseed oil
- 1 teaspoon umeboshi vinegar
- ½ cup plain unsweetened almond milk, warmed
- 2 tablespoons non-hydrogenated margarine
- 1 small bunch scallions, green part only, finely minced
- 1 teaspoon salt
  Freshly ground black pepper

1. Bring a pot of salted water to a boil and cook the potatoes until tender, 15 to 20 minutes.

2. While the potatoes are cooking, bring a large saucepan of water to a boil and cook the kale until tender, 3 to 4 minutes. Drain well and place in a large bowl. Add the oil and vinegar and toss to combine.

3. Drain the potatoes and mash well with the warm almond milk and margarine. Blend in the kale, scallions, salt, and pepper to taste. Serve hot.

Potato Pancakes with Green Scallions

SERVES 4

Scallions, or green onions, and parsley add flecks of green to these crisp fried potato pancakes. Serve them hot with cinnamon-laced applesauce or vegan sour cream. A small shredded yellow onion can be used to replace the scallions, if you prefer.

1½ pounds russet potatoes
1 bunch scallions, minced
1 tablespoon minced fresh parsley
¼ cup all-purpose flour
½ teaspoon baking powder
1 teaspoon salt
¼ teaspoon freshly ground black pepper
   Grapeseed oil, for frying

1. Peel and shred the potatoes and place them in a colander set over a large bowl. Use your hands to squeeze the liquid from the potatoes. Pour off the liquid from the potatoes and place the potatoes in the bowl. Add the scallions, parsley, flour, baking powder, salt, and pepper and mix well.

2. Preheat the oven to 275°F. Heat a thin layer of oil in a large skillet over medium heat. Press a heaping tablespoon of the potato mixture flat, then gently place in the hot oil. Repeat this process to make 3 or 4 more potato pancakes and add them to the pan. Do not crowd the pan. Fry until golden brown on both sides, turning once, 7 to 8 minutes total. Transfer the cooked potato pancakes to paper towels to drain excess oil, then transfer to an ovenproof platter and keep them warm in the oven until all the pancakes have been cooked. Add more oil to the skillet as needed while cooking the remaining pancakes.

Thyme-Scented Sweet Potatoes with Black Olives and Garlic

SERVES 4

If those awful candied sweet potatoes in a can have left you avoiding sweet potatoes at every turn, you need to try them fresh and prepared in a savory rather than sweet way. This recipe, redolent of garlic and thyme and studded with black olives, should change your mind about sweet potatoes once and for all.

1½ pounds sweet potatoes
2 tablespoons olive oil, plus more for drizzling (optional)
3 garlic cloves, crushed
1 teaspoon dried thyme
Salt and freshly ground black pepper
⅓ cup pitted oil-cured black olives

Peel the sweet potatoes, halve them lengthwise, and cut them into ¼-inch-thick slices. Heat the oil in a large skillet over medium heat. Add the sweet potatoes and garlic. Sprinkle with the thyme and season with salt and pepper to taste. Cook for 1 minute, stirring to coat. Decrease the heat to low, cover, and cook until the potatoes are tender, about 20 minutes, stirring occasionally. A few minutes before serving time, add the olives and taste to adjust the seasonings, if needed. Drizzle with a little additional olive oil, if you like.

Broccoli- and Cheddar-Stuffed Portobellos

SERVES 4

I love the cheesy broccoli filling in these stuffed mushrooms. If you can't find the very large portobellos, then serve two smaller ones per person. Enjoy these as a side dish or a main dish, or use smaller mushrooms and serve as an appetizer.

3½ cups chopped broccoli
2 tablespoons roasted red bell pepper or jarred pimientos, blotted dry
1 tablespoon beer or dry sherry
1 tablespoon cider vinegar
1 teaspoon yellow mustard
¾ cup cashews, soaked for 4 hours, then drained
2 tablespoons nutritional yeast
½ teaspoon onion powder
½ teaspoon smoked paprika
½ teaspoon salt
¼ teaspoon freshly ground black pepper
¼ teaspoon ground turmeric
2 tablespoons coconut oil, melted
2 tablespoons hot water
4 large or 8 small portobello mushroom caps
2 tablespoons soy sauce
1 teaspoon liquid smoke
2 tablespoons finely ground walnuts

1. Preheat the oven to 400°F. Lightly oil a 9- x 13-inch baking dish. Bring an inch or two of water to a boil in a pot and steam the broccoli over the water until just tender. Transfer to a bowl and let cool.

2. In a food processor or high-speed blender, combine the roasted red bell pepper, beer, vinegar, and mustard. Process until the mixture is pureed and smooth. Add the cashews, nutritional yeast, onion powder, paprika, salt, black pepper, and turmeric. Process to a paste, scraping down the sides as needed. Add the melted coconut oil and hot water and process until smooth, scraping down the sides as needed. Transfer the cheese mixture to the bowl with the broccoli and mix well.

CONTINUED ON PAGE 162

CONTINUED FROM PAGE 160

3. Heat the oil in a skillet over medium heat. Add the mushrooms and cook on both sides to soften, about 3 minutes per side. Add the soy sauce and liquid smoke and cook, flipping the mushrooms to coat. Remove from the heat and let cool, stem side down.

4. When the mushrooms are cool enough to handle, mound a portion of the broccoli mixture into each mushroom, pressing to fill the mushroom. Arrange the stuffed mushroom in the prepared baking dish. Sprinkle the top of each mushroom with the ground walnuts and bake until hot, about 20 minutes. Serve hot.

Roasted Zucchini and Tomatoes

SERVES 4

This is an adaptation of my mother's zucchini recipe that
I've enjoyed since childhood. Instead of combining the
ingredients on top of the stove, I cook them in the oven,
giving the dish an added dimension of flavor that only
comes from roasting. Whole or halved cherry or grape
tomatoes may be substituted for the larger plum tomatoes,
if desired.

1½   pounds zucchini, halved lengthwise
1½   pounds ripe plum tomatoes, quartered lengthwise
½   small yellow onion, chopped
2   garlic cloves, minced
1   tablespoon olive oil
½   teaspoon dried basil
¼   teaspoon dried oregano
    Salt and freshly ground black pepper

Preheat the oven to 400°F. Cut the zucchini into ¼-inch-thick
slices and place in a large baking dish. Cut the tomato quarters
in half crosswise and add to the baking dish along with the onion,
garlic, oil, basil, oregano, and salt and pepper to taste. Toss
well to coat the vegetables with the oil and seasonings. Roast,
uncovered, until tender, stirring once about halfway through,
30 to 40 minutes.

Sweet Endings

People are often surprised at how simple it is to prepare desserts without using eggs or dairy products. Frequently, it's as easy as making a simple ingredient swap, such as using a vegan butter such as Earth Balance in place of dairy butter, or a nondairy milk in place of dairy milk. There are many substitutes for eggs as well (see page 21), and honey is easily replaced with agave nectar or pure maple syrup.

This chapter includes many tried-and-true favorites, desserts I make most often by special request of family and friends. I hope they become your favorites as well.

Coconut Cupcakes

Maple-Walnut Oatmeal Cookies

Quick Apple Crisp

Chocolate–Almond Butter Truffles

Chocolate Faux Silk Pie

Crazy for Carrot Cake

Sour Cream Coffee Cake

Agave Baklava

Double-Chocolate Brownies

Coconut Cupcakes

MAKES 12 CUPCAKES

I developed these cupcakes especially for my husband, who loves coconut desserts. They look especially pretty with large flakes of toasted coconut sprinkled on the frosting.

CUPCAKES:
- ¾ cup coconut milk
- 1 teaspoon cider vinegar
- 1¼ cups all-purpose flour
- 2 tablespoons cornstarch
- 1 teaspoon ground nutmeg
- ½ teaspoon salt
- 1 teaspoon baking powder
- ¼ teaspoon baking soda
- ¾ cup granulated sugar
- 3 tablespoons coconut oil, melted
- 1 teaspoon coconut extract

FROSTING:
- ⅓ cup vegan butter
- 2 cups confectioners' sugar
- 1 teaspoon coconut extract
- Flaked coconut, for garnish

Cupcakes:

1. Preheat the oven to 350°F. Line a 12-cup muffin tin with cupcake liners.

2. In a small bowl, combine the coconut milk and vinegar. In a medium bowl, combine the flour, cornstarch, nutmeg, salt, baking powder, and baking soda. Mix to combine.

3. In a large bowl, combine the sugar, oil, and coconut extract. Stir in the coconut milk mixture. Add the dry ingredients to the wet ingredients and stir until smooth.

4. Pour the batter evenly into the prepared tin and bake until a toothpick inserted into the center of a cupcake comes out clean, 20 to 25 minutes. Let cool completely before frosting.

CONTINUED ON PAGE 168

CONTINUED FROM PAGE 167

Frosting:

5. While the cupcakes are cooling, in a large bowl, cream the butter with an electric mixer on high speed until light and fluffy. Alternatively, process it in a food processor. Add the confectioners' sugar and coconut extract and mix until thoroughly combined. Continue mixing for about 2 minutes, or until the frosting is smooth and stiff. Refrigerate until needed.

To assemble:

6. Frost the cooled cupcakes with the frosting. Place the flaked coconut in a shallow bowl, then dip the top of each cupcake into the coconut.

Toasting Coconut

To toast shredded or flaked coconut, preheat the oven to 325°F. Spread the coconut flakes in a thin layer on a baking sheet and bake until golden brown, stirring occasionally, 5 to 10 minutes.

Maple-Walnut Oatmeal Cookies

MAKES ABOUT 24 COOKIES

These old-fashioned favorites are loaded with the wholesome goodness of rolled oats, walnuts, and maple syrup. Dried cranberries would make a good addition for their color, flavor, and nutrients.

- 1 cup all-purpose flour
- 1 teaspoon baking powder
- 1 teaspoon ground cinnamon
- ¼ teaspoon ground nutmeg
- ⅛ teaspoon salt
- 1 cup old-fashioned rolled oats
- ¾ cup chopped walnuts
- ½ cup vegan butter or coconut oil, melted
- ½ cup pure maple syrup
- ½ cup sugar
- ¼ cup plain unsweetened almond or soy milk
- 1 teaspoon pure vanilla extract

1. Preheat the oven to 375°F. In a large bowl, combine the flour, baking powder, cinnamon, nutmeg, and salt. Stir in the oats and walnuts. In a separate bowl, combine the butter, maple syrup, sugar, almond milk, and vanilla, and mix well. Add the wet ingredients to the dry ingredients, stirring to mix well.

2. Drop the cookie dough by the tablespoonful onto an ungreased baking sheet and press down slightly with a fork. Bake until nicely browned, about 12 minutes. Let the cookies cool for a few minutes before removing from the baking sheet.

Quick Apple Crisp

SERVES 6

When you want the flavor of apple pie without the bother of a crust, this quick crisp is the way to go. Enlist some help to peel the apples and it can be in the oven in minutes.

- 5 large Granny Smith or Stayman apples (about 6 cups sliced)
- ½ cup pure maple syrup
- 1 tablespoon fresh lemon juice
- 1 teaspoon ground cinnamon
- 1 cup old-fashioned rolled oats
- ½ cup all-purpose flour
- ½ cup sugar
- ½ cup vegan butter, softened

1. Preheat the oven to 350°F. Lightly oil a 9-inch square baking pan. Peel, core, and slice the apples and place them in the pan. Drizzle the maple syrup and lemon juice over the apples and sprinkle with ½ teaspoon of the cinnamon.

2. In a bowl, mix the oats, flour, sugar, and remaining ½ teaspoon cinnamon. Cream in the butter until well mixed. Spread the topping mixture evenly over the apple mixture. Bake until bubbling and lightly browned on top, about 45 minutes. Serve warm.

Chocolate–Almond Butter Truffles

MAKES 24 TRUFFLES

The mellow buttery flavor of almonds merges with rich chocolate for a sublime treat. Serve with coffee after a special meal or to make an everyday meal special.

- 1 cup vegan semisweet chocolate chips
- ½ cup almond butter
- 2 tablespoons plain unsweetened almond or soy milk
- 1 tablespoon pure vanilla extract
- 1 cup confectioners' sugar
- 2 tablespoons unsweetened cocoa powder
- ½ cup ground toasted almonds

1. Melt the chocolate in the top of a double boiler set over simmering water or in the microwave. In a food processor, combine the almond butter, almond milk, and vanilla and blend until smooth. Add the confectioners' sugar, cocoa powder, and melted chocolate and blend until smooth and creamy. Transfer the mixture to a bowl and refrigerate for 30 minutes to chill.

2. Use your hands to roll the chilled mixture into 1-inch balls and place them on a baking sheet. Place the ground almonds in a shallow bowl and roll the balls in them, turning to coat. Place the truffles on a serving platter and refrigerate for 30 minutes before serving.

Chocolate Faux Silk Pie

SERVES 6 TO 8

The creamy texture of the filling is incomparable, and the luscious flavor is a chocolate lover's dream. This gorgeous and sophisticated dessert is easier to make than it looks, requires no baking, and is guaranteed to win rave reviews from your dinner guests.

2½ cups vegan chocolate cookies (about 15 cookies)
  2 tablespoons vegan butter or coconut oil, melted
  1 (12-ounce) bag vegan semisweet chocolate chips
  ½ cup raw cashews, soaked for 4 hours, then drained
  ⅓ cup pure maple syrup
  1 (12-ounce) package firm silken tofu, drained and patted dry
  2 teaspoons pure vanilla extract
    Sliced almonds, toasted, for garnish

1. Coat an 8-inch pie plate or springform pan with nonstick vegetable cooking spray. Break the cookies into a food processor and process until they become crumbs. Add the melted butter and pulse until the crumbs are moistened. Press the crumb mixture into the bottom and sides of the pie plate. Refrigerate until needed.

2. Melt the chocolate chips in the top of a double boiler set over simmering water or in the microwave.

3. In a high-speed blender, grind the cashews to a paste. Add the maple syrup and blend until smooth. Add the tofu and blend until creamy. Add the melted chocolate chips and vanilla and blend until smooth. Pour the filling into the prepared crust and refrigerate for 2 hours. Garnish with toasted almonds when ready to serve.

Crazy for Carrot Cake

SERVES 8

Carrot cake is a personal favorite, and everyone who's tasted this carrot cake agrees that it's the best carrot cake they've had, vegan or not. It's a rich and flavorful cake without being cloyingly sweet, moist with sweet bits of carrot and cloaked in a luscious and creamy frosting. And what a decadent way to get your beta-carotene for the day. For a bit of crunch, add ½ cup chopped walnuts. For an even richer carrot color, substitute carrot juice for all or part of the soy milk.

    2   cups all-purpose flour
    1¾ teaspoons baking powder
    2   teaspoons ground cinnamon
    1   teaspoon ground allspice
    ¾   teaspoon salt
    ¾   teaspoon baking soda
    1   cup sugar
    ½   cup plain unsweetened almond or soy milk
    ½   cup grapeseed oil
    ¼   cup pure maple syrup
    2   teaspoons pure vanilla extract
    2   cups finely grated carrots
    ½   cup golden raisins
        Cream Cheese Frosting (recipe follows)

1. Preheat the oven to 350°F. Grease a 9-inch square baking pan. In a large bowl, mix together the flour, baking powder, cinnamon, allspice, salt, and baking soda. In a medium bowl, combine the sugar, almond milk, oil, maple syrup, and vanilla, then add the wet ingredients to the dry ingredients and blend until combined. Fold in the carrots and raisins until just mixed. Spread the batter into the prepared pan.

2. Bake until a toothpick inserted into the center comes out clean, 50 to 55 minutes. Let cool on a wire rack. Loosen the edges and then invert the cake onto a serving platter. Let cool completely, then frost the cake.

CONTINUED ON PAGE 176

CONTINUED FROM PAGE 175

Cream Cheese Frosting

MAKES ABOUT 2½ CUPS

This frosting is famous for being the crowning glory of a carrot cake. Look for containers of vegan cream cheese in natural foods stores and well-stocked supermarkets.

- 1 **(8-ounce) container vegan cream cheese, softened**
- 3 **cups confectioners' sugar, or more as needed**
- 1 **teaspoon pure vanilla extract**

Combine all of the ingredients in a food processor and process until smooth. Alternatively, you may use an electric mixer to beat the ingredients until light and fluffy. If the frosting is too thin, add more confectioners' sugar. Refrigerate until needed.

Sour Cream Coffee Cake

SERVES 8 TO 10

A tube pan or Bundt pan will give this cake a classic coffee cake look, but you can also bake it in a 9- x 13-inch baking pan if that's what you've got.

- ¾ cup chopped walnuts
- 1½ teaspoons ground cinnamon
- 2 cups sugar
- 3 cups all-purpose flour
- 2 teaspoons baking powder
- 1½ teaspoons baking soda
- 1 (12-ounce) package firm silken tofu
- ½ cup grapeseed oil
- 2 teaspoons fresh lemon juice
- 1½ teaspoons pure vanilla extract
- ¾ cup vegan butter

1. Preheat the oven to 350°F. Grease a tube pan. In a small bowl, combine the walnuts, cinnamon, and ¾ cup of the sugar and set aside. In a medium bowl, sift together the flour, baking powder, and baking soda.

2. In a food processor or blender, combine the tofu, oil, lemon juice, and vanilla, and process until smooth. In a large bowl using an electric mixer, combine the butter with the remaining 1¼ cups sugar and beat until light and fluffy. Add the flour mixture and the tofu mixture and beat on low speed until blended. Increase the speed to medium and beat for 3 minutes.

3. Spread half of the nut mixture over the bottom of the prepared pan. Spread half of the batter in the pan and sprinkle with the remaining nut mixture. Spread the remaining batter evenly over the top of the nut mixture.

4. Bake until firm, about 60 minutes. When the cake is completely cool, turn it out of the pan and onto a plate.

Agave Baklava

MAKES 36 PIECES

Vegans who love baklava can rejoice: They can now enjoy their favorite phyllo treat thanks to this vegan version that replaces the dairy butter and honey with vegan butter and agave nectar. Frozen phyllo dough needs to thaw in the refrigerator (not at room temperature) for at least 6 hours. If you thaw it at room temperature, the phyllo sheets will stick together. Cutting the phyllo dough into half sheets makes it easier to work with.

- 2 cups coarsely ground walnuts
- 1 teaspoon ground cinnamon
- 1 cup sugar
- 1 (16-ounce) package phyllo dough, thawed in the refrigerator
- 1 cup vegan butter, melted
- ½ cup water
- ½ cup agave nectar
- 2 teaspoons fresh lemon juice
- 1 teaspoon pure vanilla extract

1. Preheat the oven to 350°F. Grease a 9- x 13-inch baking dish. Place the nuts, cinnamon, and ¼ cup of the sugar in a bowl and toss to combine.

2. Unroll the phyllo dough and cut the dough in half so the sheets fit the baking dish. Keep the unused phyllo covered with a damp cloth to keep it from drying out. Place half of the pastry sheets, one at a time, into the prepared baking pan, brushing each sheet with some of the melted butter. Sprinkle the nut mixture over the phyllo. Place the remaining phyllo sheets on top, brushing each with more of the melted butter. Brush the top with the remaining butter.

3. Cut the pastry into 2-inch diamonds with a sharp knife. To do this, first make three evenly spaced cuts through the length of the dough, cutting through the dough layers to the bottom of the dish, resulting in four long rows. Then make nine diagonal cuts through the shorter width of the dough. You should end up with 36 pieces of baklava. Bake until crisp and golden brown, about 45 minutes.

4. While the baklava is baking, combine the remaining ¾ cup sugar and the water in a saucepan over medium heat and bring to a boil. Decrease the heat to low and stir in the agave, lemon juice, and vanilla. Simmer until syrupy, about 20 minutes. Remove the baklava from the oven and spoon the syrup over it. Let cool completely before serving. Store uncovered.

Double-Chocolate Brownies

MAKES 12 BROWNIES

These chocolaty confections are a brownie lover's dream, with a dense, fudgy texture and rich, intense flavor. I know one chocoholic who actually topped one of these beauties with a scoop of vegan chocolate ice cream.

1½ cups all-purpose flour
¾ cup unsweetened cocoa powder
1½ teaspoons baking powder
½ teaspoon salt
1¼ cups sugar
½ cup vegan butter
⅓ cup water
2 teaspoons pure vanilla extract
⅔ cup vegan semisweet chocolate chips, melted

1. Preheat the oven to 350°F. Grease an 8-inch square baking pan. Combine the flour, cocoa powder, baking powder, and salt in a large bowl. In a separate bowl, cream together the sugar and butter. Stir in the water and vanilla and blend until smooth. Add the wet ingredients to the dry ingredients, stirring to blend. Fold in the melted chocolate chips.

2. Scrape the batter into the baking pan, and bake until the center is set, about 40 minutes. Let the brownies cool before serving.

Index

C